Augustine's Confessions

a guide for the uninitiated

edited by
Michael S. Russo

ISBN: 9781686506475

SophiaOmni

Visit our website at:
www.sophiaomni.org

Contents

**"You have made us for yourself,
and our hearts are restless
until they rest in you."**

— *Confessions,* 1.1

Preface

The *Confessions* of St. Augustine, written in 397 A.D., is without a doubt the most important text of one of the most influential Christian writers who ever lived. Both Catholic and Protestant Christians throughout the centuries have looked to Augustine for inspiration, guidance, and justification for their beliefs. In general, when it comes to Christian thought, if Augustine said it, it's taken as authoritative by most Christians. If you want to understand the development of Christian thought, therefore, you *need* to understand Augustine.

The problem is that the complete cannon of Augustine's thought is vast and much of his later writing is quite technical in nature—more suitable for scholars of late antiquity than for the average reader. Just try reading some of Augustine's later writings on predestination and divine foreknowledge and your head will swim.

Fortunately, there's no significant idea in the entire body of Augustine's writings that can't be found in one form or another in the *Confessions*, his most famous and influential work. More importantly still, the ideas contained in the *Confessions* are presented in a way that makes them much more accessible to the average reader than other equally important and comprehensive works of his—most notably *On the Trinity* and the *City of God.* In the *Confessions*, Augustine uses his own life and his own struggles to present his ideas on grace, election, original sin, and the mystical experience in a way that is both engaging and emotionally compelling.

This is not to say that the *Confessions* does not pose problems for the twenty-first century reader. Augustine lived in a world very different from our own, and his writing reflects that reality.

The Roman Empire during the 4th century was in the midst of an intellectual and social revolution as profound as any witnessed in the history of the world. The Emperor Constantine had only legitimized Christianity in 313, a mere 84 years before the *Confessions* was written. Prior to that, if you were a Christian in the Empire, the threat of persecution always hung over your head. Furthermore, it was only between 382 and 393—roughly the same time that Augustine was undergoing his conversion—that the Emperor Theodosius issued his decrees that effectively turned Catholic Christianity into the state religion throughout the Empire. The world Augustine inhabited was one, therefore, in which the classical world was giving way to the Medieval world and the culturally and intellectually diverse Roman Empire was being transformed into a much more monolithic Christian empire.

We should also not forget that within Augustine's own lifetime, in 410 A.D., the holy city of Rome was sacked by the Visigoths, causing no small amount of anxiety for faithful Christians throughout the Empire. The danger of Germanic invasion was always hanging over the heads of the inhabitants of Italy and North Africa during the fifth century, when Augustine was at the peak of his fame. Indeed, just before his death in 430, the Vandals had begun their invasion of his own city of Hippo in North Africa. Augustine literally could look outside his window and see the whole world that he knew falling apart around him. The seemingly eternal Roman Empire which had endured for centuries would collapse completely in 476 A.D., less than half a century after Augustine's own death. Augustine, therefore, stands as a bridge between the classical world with all its intellectual optimism and the Medieval Christian world with its significantly more somber views on human sinfulness and divine judgment.

It also should be noted that Augustine wrote the way that any serious fourth century rhetorician and Christian apologist would write, which presents its own problems for the contemporary reader. He wrote in Latin, of course, the intellectual language of the Empire, and his writing style when translated too faithfully into English can come across as a bit cumbersome to the contemporary reader. He's also writing for an audience well versed in scripture, and subsequently he feels compelled to couch his ideas in biblical language. This can often make for tiresome reading for those who might not be quite as delighted by line after line of scriptural citations that often serve to break up the flow of his narrative. In short, Augustine was a writer perfectly suited to the world in which he lived, but one admittedly less well suited to our own.

That's where this little study guide comes in.

The title, *Augustine's* Confessions: *A Guide for the Uninitiated*, probably gives some idea about the scope of this work. Yes, you will find the text of Augustine's *Confessions* contained here, but you won't find the whole text and what you will find represents a looser and more fluid translation of the original text than you'll probably encounter elsewhere. This edition, in other words, is for the uninitiated—for those without any background at all in the thought of St. Augustine or with Christian doctrine in general. The goal here is to highlight the important ideas contained in the text without getting bogged down in the kind of early Medieval ruminations that can be off-putting to the contemporary reader.

There are also said to be over a thousand biblical quotes in the standard Latin edition of the text. While Augustine's fourth century audience probably would have welcomed his skillful weaving of scripture into the narrative of his life, for most of us today the results probably amount to overkill. In this edition, scriptural references remain only when they help elucidate the meaning of Augustine's point in the text, and quotation marks are used only when Augustine intentionally highlights specific passages of scripture.

In short, I've chopped out the slow-going parts of the *Confessions* and tried to modernize the language of what's left to convey what I believe to be the essence of the text. In this edition, you won't even find the last three books of the *Confessions*—Augustine's exegesis on the Book of Genesis—because very few people read these books any more . . . and for good reason.

In other words, "decisions were made"—for better or worse, depending upon your own perspective.

Consider this edition an appetizer. The aim is to give the novice reader a palatable introduction to the thought of St. Augustine as contained in his most influential and compelling work. Having recognized the depth of the great man's vision, it's my sincere hope that the reader will begin his or her own exploration of other works by St. Augustine and perhaps even be inspired to read the *Confessions* in its entirety.

Introduction

Since this is a study guide for the uninitiated, there's some background information that might help with your reading of the *Confessions*. I've included only what's absolutely necessary to get you started, allowing Augustine's text the honor of speaking for itself. Those requiring additional information about Augustine's life or the ideas contained in the *Confessions* are invited to explore the "For Further Reading" section at the back of this text.

Who Was St. Augustine?

Although the *Confessions* is in one sense an autobiographical work, Augustine tends to be selective about what information he chooses to reveal about himself to the reader. The account of his life also only goes up to 387 A.D., when Augustine was only 33 years old. Since he died at the age of 76 in 430, that means that more than half his life is not included in the *Confessions*. A brief summary of his life, therefore, seems appropriate.

Aurelius Augustinus was born on November 13, 354 A.D. in Thagaste (in modern Algeria). This region of North Africa had been an important part of the Roman Empire for some 500 years and was heavily latinized in both culture and language. Augustine was born into a respectable but impoverished family. His father Patricius was a pagan (he eventually converted before his death) and his mother, Monica, a devout Christian.

With the help of a wealthy patron, his family managed to send him to Madura, a nearby university town, so that he could continue his education. Obviously, he demonstrated a great deal potential as a student, because soon afterwards he went to Carthage (one of the great cities of North Africa) to pursue more advanced studies in rhetoric.

Augustine moved steadily up the ladder of success. After a brief but unhappy stint teaching in Rome, in 384 he was awarded a position as professor of rhetoric in Milan. Milan at this time was the *de facto* capital of the Roman Empire, since this was where the imperial court was housed. It was while he was in Milan that Augustine fell under the spell of Ambrose, the Catholic Bishop of that city and one of the main proponents of Christian Neo-Platonism. In August of 386 Augustine had a conversion experience and decided to embrace a life within the Church. Giving up his career in rhetoric (and all the promises of future success that such a life promised), he decided to return to Thagaste with his mother and his friends. While waiting in Ostia for a boat back to Africa, his mother Monica died suddenly.

Augustine's many talents were immediately recognized within the church and he was soon forced to become a priest in city of Hippo. In 396 he was made bishop of that city and would remain in the position for the next 35 years. He died on August 28, 430, just as the Roman Empire in North Africa was collapsing due to the invasion of the Vandals.

Augustine wrote numerous works on Catholic philosophy and theology with over 100 works credited to him. His most famous works, however, are the *Confessions,* an autobiographical account of his early life and conversion, *On the Trinity*, a groundbreaking work of Christian theology, and the *City of God,* which he wrote as Rome was falling to the barbarians. Most of Augustine's works were attempts to respond to the numerous heretical sects (particularly the Manichaeans, Donatists and Pelagians) that were creeping up at the time. In responding to these heresies Augustine formulated the Church's position on such important doctrines as grace, original sin and election. His contributions to the intellectual life of the Church were recognized after his death, when he was given the title "Doctor of Grace."

What Are the Confessions?

When the word "confession" comes to mind, you might be inclined to think about some sorrowful penitent spilling out his sins to a priest in a dark confessional box. But the Latin *confiteri*, from which our English word is derived, has a much broader connotation than this. In *The Young Augustine*, John J. O'Meara has argued that Augustine uses the term in three distinct but interrelated senses in the *Confessions*—as confession of sins (*confessio peccati*), confession of praise (*confessio laudis*), and confession of faith (*confessio fidei*).

It is generally held that Augustine composed his *Confessions* between 397 and 401, not long after he had been made Bishop of Hippo. In the most basic sense, the work is an autobiographical account of Augustine's early years, written from the perspective of someone looking back both on his numerous faults, but also the great blessings that God has bestowed upon him. And yet it's clear that the *Confessions* is only superficially an autobiography in the traditional sense of the term. Augustine sees himself as a kind of everyman and uses his own life and struggles as a kind of road-map illustrating the path of salvation.

But what exactly is Augustine trying to persuade his reader about, using his own life as an example?

It's evident that the question of happiness lies at the heart of the *Confessions*. In the very first chapter of the work, Augustine sets the tone for the entire text when he acknowledges that the human heart is restless until it rests in God. There's a tension throughout the work between Augustine's "unquiet," "restless," "storm-tossed" days prior to his salvation and the vision of an eternal rest that he finds in God.

The *Confessions* at its core is the story of a misguided soul seeking happiness in all the wrong places—in sensual pleasure, heresy, and secular wisdom. It is the story of a wounded heart longing for a love that will inebriate it and compel it to forsake its illicit desires. In a nutshell, it is the story of a wayward pilgrim trying to find the right way to achieve the happiness for which he so desperately longs.

But what is that "right way"?

In the *Confessions*, Augustine clearly believes that there are two very different paths that human beings can take on their journey through life. The first, exemplified by arrogant philosophers like the Neo-Platonists and misguided heretics like the Manichae-ans, is the way of presumption, in which one may recognize the goal of life (happiness in this life and beyond), but fails to under-stand the right way to reach that goal. This approach presumes that happiness can be attained by one's own effort through the proper use of reason.

The second approach is that of confession, in which one un-derstands both the goal of life and the means needed to attain that goal. This is the path of the humble—the path of one who recog-nizes his or her own limitations, and seeks the guidance of legiti-mate authority (the Church) and the assistance of a higher power (the grace of Christ). In the *Confessions*, Augustine makes it clear that it is only through the Church and only through the meditating assistance of Christ that one can be saved.

So, we now have a fourth meaning of confession that is key to understanding the central purpose of Augustine's work. The term confession can be used, not just as a verb, suggesting some activ-ity of the soul (i.e., praising, accusing, or testifying), but also as a state of being, an existential orientation, which is the opposite of presumption.

Outline of the Confessions

Great works typically have great unity of structure. If that's the case, then we are in deep trouble when it comes to the *Confes-sions*. On the surface, *Confessions* is something of a literary mon-strosity, lacking any intrinsic interconnectedness.

Let's start with the overall structure of the *Confessions*, which can be divided into three discernible parts. Books 1-9 represent the autobiographical portion of the work, with Augustine the Bishop looking back over his life from infancy until the death of his mother and his return home to North Africa. Book 10 is a bit of a mishmash, with Augustine offering a philosophical account of the nature of memory and then focusing on the present state of his soul as Bishop of Hippo. Books 11-13 are an extended exe-gesis of the "Book of Genesis" that includes almost no personal information at all.

Books 11-13 have typically presented commentators with

a conundrum, since the tone, style, and content of these books doesn't seem at all to fit what preceded them. There are those who have argued that the work may have originally been envisioned in three parts focused on the past (Books 1-9), present (Book 10), and future eternal life (Books 11-13). While this may be a neat way to tie the work together, we have no way of knowing whether this organization of the work is accurate, since Augustine is silent on the subject.

Because the first nine books of the *Confessions* work so well together as an account of Augustine's conversion, many teachers of the text have focused on those books to the exclusion of the last four. I've included parts of Book 10, because I think that it is important for understanding Augustine's ideas on the pervasiveness of worldly temptation, even in the life of those already saved by God's grace.

The division of the text that you'll find here reflects my own approach to teaching the *Confessions* and has been influenced by the stages of mystical progress developed by Evelyn Underhill in her work *Mysticism*.

1. The first part of the text (1.1-1.3) describes the effects of original sin on Augustine's life and the resulting personal sins that leave him "a wasteland unto [him]self."

2. The second part (3.4-6.5) represents Augustine's intellectual illumination—his growing understanding of the nature of God and human beings' relationship to God.

3. But intellectual illumination only can take Augustine so far. His soul must be inflamed with the love of God, so that he can overcome all the worldly desires that tempt him. So, the fourth part of the text centers on the process of moral purgation (6.6-8.12), which culminates in Augustine's famous conversion account in *Confessions* 8.12.

4. Conversion, however, is a means, not an end in itself. The end for the Christian is the mystical experience—the vision of God in this life that is but a taste of the perfect beatitude that awaits him in the next, and which sustains the believer in the midst of all the temptations and sufferings of this life. Thus, the final part of the text (9.1-10.42) deals with

mystical union and its aftermath.

This subdivision of the *Confessions* into four parts, I believe, is a helpful way to understand the some of the main themes running through the text. In the "Related Readings" section at the back of this text, you'll find additional sources that are provided to shed light on these and other significant themes in the text.

AUGUSTINIAN TIME-LINE

325	Council of Nicaea | Formulation of Nicene Creed
354	Augustine born in Thagaste in North Africa (November 13)
365	Goes to school in Madaura
371	Studies rhetoric in Carthage
372	Becomes a Manichaean auditor | Birth of Augustine's Son, Adeodatus | Death of Augustine's father, Patrick
373	Reads Cicero's *Hortensius*
374	Teaches rhetoric in Thagaste
376	Begins teaching rhetoric in Carthage
380	Emperor Theodosius makes Christianity the state religion
383	Goes to Rome to teach rhetoric
384	Becomes professor of rhetoric in Milan | Encounters the "Books of the Platonists"
386	Converted | Retreats to Cassiciacum | Writes *The Happy Life, On Order*
387	Vision at Ostia | Death of Monica
390	Returns to Africa | Death of Adeodatus
391	Ordained a priest at Hippo
395	Ordained Assistant Bishop of Hippo | Writes *On Christian Doctrine* | Completes *On the Freedom of the Will*
396	Made Bishop of Hippo
397	Begins writing the *Confessions* (completed c. 400)
413–426	Writes *The City of God, On the Trinity*, and *The Enchiridion*
429	The Vandals invade North Africa from Spain
430	Dies at Hippo (August 28) | Vandals besiege Hippo
475	Fall of the Roman Empire in the West

Becoming a Wasteland: The Great Burden of Sin

Confessions 1.1 - 3.3

─⟨⎯

In Book 1-3 of the *Confessions*, Augustine describes his infancy, childhood, and adolescence in North Africa. Whereas we typically think of infants and young children as innocents, Augustine is determined to show that this is most certainly not the case, using himself as the example. The pervasive feature in the life of all human beings is original sin, a penalty inherited from Adam and Eve. Because of this penalty, it is inevitable human beings will sin and that they will show evidence of their sinful tendencies from the moment of birth. The situation is made even worse by personal sins committed after the age of reason, for which we bear moral responsibility and therefore are deserving of punishment. Punishment for these sins is the suffering that our own moral disorders causes us in this life, but also the possibility of eternal punishment in the next life. While this perspective on human nature may seem bleak to the contemporary reader, for Augustine, the reality of our fallen natures provides the possibility of liberation from sin, which comes from the grace of God.

The *Confessions* opens with Augustine's prayer extolling the goodness of God and the sinfulness of human beings. Augustine is convinced that the person who is separated from God through his own sinfulness can never be fully happy. "You have made us for yourself," he writes, "and our hearts will remain restless until they can rest in you."[1.1] This contrast between restlessness and peace is one that will come up repeatedly in the *Confessions*. The soul, he believes, longs for peace, but can only find peace by resting in God.

Augustine is born in Thagaste (present day Algeria in North Africa) in 354 to Patricius and Monica. He begins his description of his own infancy by reflecting on the life of infants in general. He observes that a natural order has been ordained by God between mother and child, disputing the idea that there is such a thing as the innocence of infancy or childhood. From the moment of birth, the life of the infant, and later of the child, is characterized by disordered inclinations and desires that are only controlled by the prudent disciplinary actions of the child's parents. Children left to their own devices, and without proper checks on their actions, would inevitably end up causing tremendous harm to themselves and others around them. This tendency towards moral disorder, he believes, is the inevitable consequence of original sin.

Infancy gives way to childhood with the arrival of speech. During the years 365-369 Augustine begins his education in the neighboring town of Madura. If we take him seriously in the *Confessions*, his childhood education was anything but idyllic. He was often beaten for not learning his lessons to the satisfaction of his instructors.

In Book 2 Augustine recounts his further descent into moral disorder during his adolescent years. By the time that a youth reaches adolescence, and becomes conscious of the demands of the moral law, his sins take on a far more troubling dimension than they previously had: whereas the child cannot be held personally accountable for his sins, the adolescent, by freely and consciously choosing to transgress God's law, incurs a far greater penalty for his transgressions than he previously would have incurred.

In what appears to be an almost innocuous event,[2.4-2.6] Augustine aptly demonstrates the implications of personal sin in his recounting the theft of some pears during his adolescent years. On the surface the event seems harmless enough: the young Augustine and his friends stop in a neighbor's orchard and steal some of his pears. They stole the pears, he writes, not because they were hungry, but simply for the sake of taking them and afterwards threw them to the pigs to eat. Although, on the surface, Augustine's guilt over such a minor transgression might seem excessive, we can read this story as a kind of symbolic representation of all human sinfulness. What makes Augustine's act so bad is that he has now reached the age of reason and he clearly has some idea of what is right and wrong. He knows that God's law prohibits theft of any kind, and yet he steals anyway. His real sin is not theft, but pride—thinking that he is above God and his law.[2.5 -2.6]

Where has Augustine's pride gotten him? As we shall see his tendency to sin is starting to become habitual, and soon he will not be able to stop himself from doing what he clearly knows is wrong. He is, in short, on the path to becoming a "wasteland to himself."[2.10]

This downward spiral of sin and guilt reaches its climax in Book 3 of the *Confessions*. During the years 371-374 Augustine was sent to Carthage—a much larger city with greater resources—to finish his education, which centered on the study of rhetoric. In the ancient world, the mastery of this discipline was seen as a means for young men with limited resources to improve their station in life.

The city of Carthage was approximately a two days journey from his home-town of Thagaste and filled with all the temptations of any big city. He has casual sexual relations with nameless women.[3.1] and develops "unfriendly friendships" with an unsavory bunch of young men (the "Subverters"). Being ambitious, however, he never allows these relationships to interfere with his studies.[3.3]

Related Readings

Augustine. "Human Happiness"
Augustine. "Original Sin"
Augustine. "The Right Order of Loves"

BOOK 1

Opening Prayer [1.1–1.5]

1. You are great, my Lord, and immensely worthy of praise. Your power is supreme and your wisdom beyond all measure. We human beings, who are part of your creation, desire to praise you— we who carry our own mortality about us as a consequence of sin and proof that you resist the proud. But we, though just a small part of your creation, still long to sing your praises. You move us to delight in praising you, for you have made us for yourself, and our hearts are restless until they rest in you.

Lord, teach me to know and understand which should come first: To know you or to praise you? To know you or to call upon you? But how can one call upon you who is ignorant of you, since one who doesn't know you might be calling upon something other than you. Or should we instead pray to you, so that we might come to know you? But how can people call upon you, if they don't yet believe in you? . . .

2. And how shall I call upon you, my God, my Lord and my God, since the very act of calling upon you would mean calling you into myself? And what place is there in me that is fit for you to come—you who made the heavens and the earth? Is there any place in me, Lord, that can contain you? Can even the heavens and the earth, which you have made, and in which you have made me, contain you? Or, since nothing at all could exist without you, doesn't it follow that whatever exists contains you? But if this is so, why do I ask you to enter me, since, unless you were already in me, I would not even exist? . . .

Why then do I even bother to call out to you when I am already in you? Or where can you come from to enter me? Where outside of heaven and earth could I possibly travel so that you might come into me—you who have proclaimed, "I fill heaven and the earth." . . .

4. What then are you my God, but the Lord God. For who is Lord but the Lord, and who is God but God. You are the supreme, the most excellent, the most powerful, the most merciful and the most just, the most totally hidden yet most completely present,

the most beautiful and the most strong, ever constant yet incomprehensible, unchanging yet the source of all change, never new, never old, renewing all things, . . . always acting yet always at rest, ... creating, nurturing, and protecting everything, ever seeking, and yet in need of nothing.

You love, but without passion; you are jealous, but without fear; you have regret, but without sorrow. Even in your anger, you are calm. You change your works, but never your plans; you take back what you find, although you've never lost anything; you rejoice in your gains, although you're never in need; you're never greedy, although you always claim profit . . . And in all this, what I have said, my God, my life, my holy sweetness? What can anyone actually say who tries to speak of you? Yet how sad those are who don't speak of you at all, when those who speak the most say absolutely nothing.

5. How shall I find rest in you? Who shall send you into my heart to intoxicate it, allowing me to forget my own evils and embrace you as my one and only good? What are you to me? Have mercy on me so that I might speak to you. What am I to you that you should command me to love you, and that you should be angry with me and threaten me with misery if I don't love you? Isn't the failure to love you in itself misery enough? Such sorrow! Tell me in your great mercy, O Lord my God, what you are to me. Say to my soul, "I am your salvation." Say it so I can hear it . . . Don't hide your face from me . . .

The dwelling place that is my soul is much too cramped for you. Expand it, so that you might enter it. It is in ruins, so repair it. I confess that it must surely contain things that must offend your eyes. But who will cleanse the house of my soul? To whom but you should I cry out: Cleanse me, Lord, from my deepest sins and deliver your servant from the power of evil. You know all things, Lord. Haven't I confessed my sins to you, and haven't you forgiven the wickedness of my heart? I don't presume to argue my case before you, since you are Truth itself . . . Were you to keep count of the sum of all human sins, who could possibly stand it?

The "Sins" of Infancy [1.6–1.7]

6. So, let me speak to your mercy, even though I'm just dust and

ashes. Let me speak, for it is to you that I speak and not to one who would mock me. Even though you may smile upon me, I know that you will turn and have compassion upon me.

What I want to say, Lord, is this—that I don't know how it is that I came into this life. Shall I call it a dying life or a living death? I don't know where I came from. Though I can't remember it myself, I know from my parents, through whom you formed me, that I was welcomed into this world by your tender mercies. The comforts of a woman's milk sustained me. But neither my mother nor my nurses filled their own breasts with milk. Rather it was you, through them, who provided me with the nourishment of my infancy, according to your order and from the riches contained in your creation. You also made me desire to suck no more than you supplied and moved those who nurtured me to give to me what you gave them. You inspired them to share with me a portion of the bounty that you granted to them—a blessing . . . which came through rather than from them, since all true blessings come from you, my God. This fact I came to know only later, when you revealed yourself to me . . . At that time all I knew how to do was suck, be satisfied with what pleased me, and cry out at what pained me, but nothing more.

Afterwards, I also began to smile—at first only in my sleep, but later also when awake. So I have been told, and I can believe it, because we see other infants doing so too, though I don't remember it. And then, little by little, I began to become conscious of where I was and developed the ability to tell my needs to those who might satisfy them. But, of course, I couldn't yet clearly express myself to them, for my desires were inside me and they were outside, and they could not enter into the workings of my mind. So I would thrash my limbs about and make various noises, as well as I could, to indicate what I wanted. And when others didn't do what I wanted—either because they didn't understand me or because they recognized that what I wanted was harmful to me—then I would become enraged at my elders for not being completely subservient to me and others for having the audacity to act as though they weren't my slaves. And I would take my revenge upon them all by crying. I know that infants are like this, because I have been able to observe them. They, in their ignorance, have shown me what I was like as an infant, far better than the nurses who knew me so well . . .

7. Hear me, Lord, as I weep for the sins of humankind. A person regrets his sins, and you have mercy upon him, because you have created him, though not, of course, the sin in him. Who is there to remind me of the sins of my infancy? For in your sight there is no one free of sin, not even the infant who has lived on the earth a single day. Who will remind me of those sins? Certainly, every little one bears the proof of this, since I can see this for myself, even though I don't remember it personally.

What was my sin, then? Was it that I cried out so greedily for more after the milk from those breasts? Imagine if I behaved that way today, crying out, not of course for the milk of the breast, but food more suitable for my own age! I would rightly be mocked and treated with contempt for such behavior. My behavior back then was also deserving of reprimand, but, because I could not understand anyone who would rebuke me, neither custom nor reason would have allowed me to be blamed. For, as we grow up we naturally root out and cast away such childish practices.

. . . Should certain typical forms of behavior in an infant, as I once was, be regarded as good? For example, crying to get what get what I desired, even if getting it would be harmful to me? Getting angry when people who were responsible for me—my elders and my parents—didn't do exactly as I wanted. Fighting ferociously with various others who wouldn't give in to my demands, even though in doing so they have caused harm to me? It is evident that the innocence of an infant lies in the weakness of its body, not in any innocence of mind. I myself have seen and observed the jealousy of a baby; it wasn't even able to speak, yet turned blue with bitterness at another baby sharing its milk. Everyone has seen this sort of behavior, and mothers and nurses claim that they have certain ways of appeasing such infants. But can it really be called "innocence" when a baby, completely fed, won't allow another child to share its food, even when that other child is in greater need and requires such nourishment in order to survive? We put up with this, not because we don't regard the behavior as faulty . . . , but because we assume that the behavior will change as the child grows older. This is evident from the fact that we wouldn't tolerate this type of behavior in an older person . . .

I confess that I have no memory of this period of my life, Lord.

All I know is what I heard from others and from inference, however unreliable, from observing the behavior of other infants. But I'm reluctant to link that phase of my life to the life I now live in the world. In the murky mists of forgetfulness, this period of life might as well be the same as the one I spent in my mother's womb. But, if I was formed in disorder and, if my mother conceived me in sin, where or when, Lord, was I, your servant, ever truly innocent?

But I'll pass over that time. After all, what does it have to do with me now, since I can't even recall a single memory from the period of infancy?

The "Sins" of Childhood [1.8–1.20]

8. Eventually, I grew out of the state of infancy and into childhood. Or should I rather say that childhood grew into me and replaced infancy? For my infancy didn't simply disappear. Where would it go? But it wasn't any longer with me, since I was no longer an infant without speech, but a chattering boy.

I remember this and later observed how I first learned to speak. For my elders did not teach me to speak through any formal methods, as they would later on. Rather, I learned to speak using the mind that you gave me, Lord. Through various sorts of gruntings, noises, and gestures, I made myself understood to others and expressed what I wanted. I learned to repeat words through memory. When people around me called an object by a certain name, saying the word and pointing to the thing, I would remember the sounds they used to indicate the thing they wanted. Their meaning was clear to me, since they used bodily gestures as a kind of natural language, such as the glance of an eye, movements of particular limbs, and specific tone of voice—all of which indicated a certain tendency of the mind as it seeks out what it wants to possess and rejects what it wants to avoid.

So it happened that, by constantly hearing words placed in their proper order in sentences, I came to understand what these words meant. And, learning to utter these same words, I eventually was able to express what I wanted to express and to convey my own needs to others. In this way, I began to wade into the stormy world of human affairs, although I was still dependent upon the authority of parents and the commands of my elders.

9. O my God, what miseries and abuses I experienced in my childhood! I was told, at that time, that I ought to obey those who taught me how to advance in the world and to excel in the arts of speech, which would enable me to gain prestige among men and dubious riches. And so I was sent to school to learn, although I couldn't see the point of such learning. But if I failed to excel in my learning, I was beaten—a practice deemed beneficial by our ancestors and those who had gone before us....

But, Lord, we also saw people praying to you. From them we formed an impression of you . . . as a great being, who was able to hear us and help us, even when not present to our senses. So, as a young boy, I began to pray to you, my help and refuge. In doing so, I broke through the limitations of language and begged you— in my small-boy way, but with no small amount of earnestness— not to let me be beaten at school. Of course, you didn't respond to my prayers, not wanting to encourage me in my foolishness. These beatings, which were a great misery to me, were laughed at by my elders, and even by my parents, who certainly wished me no harm.

When I think about the various torments that were afflicted upon us by our masters, and how our parents used to laugh about them, I wonder if there is anyone at all with a great spirit of love for you, Lord, . . . who can look upon the racks and hooks of education as anything other than a form of torture that people all over the world pray to you to be spared. In truth, we were just as terrified of our torments and prayed no less to you to be freed of them. And yet we sinned by working less diligently on our writing, reading, and our daily lessons than was expected of us. It was not, Lord, that we lacked the memory or intelligence, which you had granted us in abundance for our age. But we delighted only in play, and for this we were punished by those adults who amused themselves by behaving exactly in the same way. But, whereas the idleness of adults is called 'business,' children who behave likewise are punished for their behavior. And neither the child nor the adult receives any pity. I question whether any reasonable judge would think that it was just for me to be beaten for playing ball, because in doing so I was I was hindering the studies which would enable me to play even more unsavory games later on in life. And was the teacher who beat me any better him-self—a teacher, who, when triumphed over by a colleague in an argument, was far more bitter and tormented than I ever was when beaten by a friend on the playground?

10. And yet I sinned, my Lord God, . . . in not obeying the commands of my parents and teachers. For later on in life, I might have put good use to the learning they wished me to acquire, whatever their motivations in wanting me to do so. In reality, I didn't disobey them because I had chosen a better path for myself, but because of my love for play, the thrill of victory in games, and the delight in being enticed by false stories, the hearing of which caused me to become all the more enticed . . . Look down mer-cifully, Lord, upon these things, and save us who now call upon you. Save also those who do not call upon you, so that you can free them as well.

11. While still a boy, I heard about the eternal life promised to us through the humility of your son, our Lord . . . My mother placed great trust in you, and, as soon as I came out of the womb, I was signed with the Lord's cross and seasoned with his salt. You saw, Lord, how, when I was still a boy, I was seized with pain in my stomach and brought close to the point of death. You saw this, my God, because you were already my guardian. You saw with what deep devotion I turned to my mother and to your Church, the mother of us all, and pleaded for the baptism of your Christ, my Lord and my God. And my mother, . . . deeply concerned, . . . made preparations [for me to be baptized] and washed clean by confessing to you, in the event that I didn't recover. When I did recover, my baptism was deferred, since it was believed that, as I continued on in life, I would become all the more defiled, since the guilt incurred by the stain of sin was far greater after baptism than before. This was what I believed at the time, as did my moth-er and our whole household, except my father who . . . had not yet become a believer . . .

I ask you, my God, to explain to me—for I would like to know, if you would tell me—what was the reason that my baptism was put off at that time? Was it for my own good that the reigns of sin were slackened for me? . . . Even now we hear people all around saying of another person, "Let him alone. Let him do what he wants. He's not baptized yet, anyway." And yet, when it comes to the health of the body, we don't say, "Let him go on injuring himself. He's not well yet, anyway." How much better would it have been for me to have been cured all at once, so that by my own diligence and that of my friends, my soul would have been kept safe in the care of you, who gave it to me. This definitely would have been far better. Instead, wave upon wave of temptations seemed to be towering over me after boyhood. My mother had foreseen these dangers and preferred to risk them in [the state I was in now rather than after baptism].

12. As a child . . . I was compelled to study, and this was in fact a good thing for me, although I wasn't the one who was responsible for this. In fact, I would never have learned anything had I not been forced to do so; and no one can act well against his own inclinations, even if what he does is good in itself. Those who were compelling me to study weren't acting very well either. Rather, the good that was done to me came through you. For my teachers had no idea how I was to use the education that they had forced upon me, except for the accumulation of wealth—a rich sort of poverty and a dishonorable glory, indeed. But you . . . made use of the errors of those who forced me to learn for my own good, and likewise made use of my own error in not wanting to learn to punish me. And I certainly deserved this punishment, being so great a sinner for such a small boy. Therefore, through the use of those who were not acting so well, you did well by me, and through my own sins, punished me. For you have ordained that every disordered desire should be its own form of punishment.

13. I still don't understand why I so hated the Greek I was force to study as a boy. Latin, on the other hand, I loved very much—not so much the more rudimentary part taught by my elementary school teachers, but the literature that the masters taught. For the more basic studies of reading, writing, and arithmetic were no less painful and difficult for me than the study of Greek. And the only reason for this was because of the sin of pride . . . In fact, the earlier lessons were definitely more profitable than the latter, because they were more reliable, having given me a power that I still retain—the ability to read anything I come across and the write about whatever is on my mind. The latter studies, on the other hand, only compelled me to memorize accounts of the wanderings of some fellow named Aeneas, while forgetting myself,

and caused me to weep over the death of Dido, who killed herself for love, while at the same time, I—fool that I was—never shed a tear as I died in my relationship with you, O God my life!

What indeed could possibly be more pitiful than a pathetic individual who has no pity for himself, weaping at the death of Dido for love . . . , and not weeping at his own death, brought about by not loving you, O God? . . . I did not love you and strayed from you, while all around me people shouted, "Nice work! Well done!" For the lust for this world is fornication against you . . .

But let my God cry out in my soul and tell me in truth that... the elementary learning I received was far better. For certainly I would rather forget everything about the wanderings of Aeneas, and all things of this sort, than how to read or write . . . For, if it were asked, which would cause the greater harm if it were forgotten, reading and writing or the fictitious tales of the poets, could we possibly doubt which answer would be given by anyone in his right mind?

So I sinned, therefore, as a boy when I preferred those more frivolous studies to more profitable ones—or rather should I say that I loved the former and hated the latter. At that time "One and one makes two; two and two makes four" was a horrible jingle to me, while the wooden horse filled with armed warriors, the burning of Troy, and the ghostly shadow of Creusa filled me with delight . . .

17. Allow me, my God, to say something about my intelligence—your gift to me—and how I wasted it upon frivolous pursuits. I recall how my teacher set before me the task of . . . reciting a speech supposedly made by Juno, expressing both her anger and frustration at not being able to keep the Trojan king from going off to Italy. I was told that Juno, in fact, never uttered these words, yet nonetheless we were forced to turn into prose the poetical fictions that the poet had written in verse. And the boy who won the most applause was he who was best able to aptly clothe the emotions of anger and frustration as befitting the character of the one being represented.

How did it benefit me, O God and my true life, that my speech was applauded more than most of those who were my own age and my fellow students. All this is just smoke and wind. Was there no other subject upon which I could exercise my intelligence and my tongue? But of course there was: Your praise, O Lord—praise recounted in scripture that might have supported the tender shoots of my soul, so it would not have produced a droopy yield fit only for flying scavengers. For there are more ways than one to sacrifice to fallen angels.

18. It is no wonder that I was carried away by vanities and estranged from you, O my God, considering the models set up for me to imitate. Such men would be criticized and ashamed of themselves for relating some action of theirs, not at all bad, using some sort of crude and irregular forms of speech; but if they recounted some tale of their lusts in proper and ornate style, with well-chosen words, they were accorded full praise and honor . . . Look down patiently, Lord, as you always do, on how obsessively the sons of men follow the proper rules for use of letters and syllables, which they have received from those who came before them, and yet neglect the eternal rules of everlasting salvation, received from you. Indeed, if a speaker, wishing to follow proper pronunciation, were to say *hominem* (man) without articulating the "h" in the first syllable, in contradiction to the rules of grammar, he would offend more people than if he, a human being, were to hate another human being, in contradiction to your commandments . . .

19. This was the situation in which I, an unhappy boy, found myself. This was the arena in which I was struggling—one in which I was terrified of committing any sort of barbarism of speech . . . These are the things I tell to you, my God, in my confession, and these are the things for which I was applauded by those I sought to please, for I didn't yet grasp the terrible chasm that I had been cast into, far out of your sight. In your eyes, what could be more terrible that what I already was. I was even beginning to earn the disapproval of those near to me—my tutor, my masters, and my parents—with my innumerable deceptions, my love of play, my desire to see vain shows, and my frivolous desire to imitate what I saw in those shows.

I stole from my parents' cellar and table too, either out gluttony or just to have something to give to other boys for the cherished trinkets they were willing to trade with me. In such games as these, I often sought to cheat my friends out of a desire to dominate them. But I would attack others in the most forceful language for doing just as I was doing, if I caught them in the act. And when

I was caught cheating, and attacked for it, I preferred to argue rather than to admit that I was wrong.

Is this what is referred to as "the innocence of childhood"? It is not, O Lord; it definitely is not. I beg your mercy, O God, for these same sins are magnified as we grow older. Then, they are directed not towards tutors and masters, nuts and balls, and sparrows, but to magistrates and kings, gold, land and slaves . . .

31. But, Lord, even if it had been your will that I didn't live beyond childhood, I would still give you thanks, O most excellent and good architect and ruler of the universe. For I existed then; I lived and felt, and was concerned about my own welfare . . . I kept watch over my outer senses by my inner sense, and even in the trifling thoughts I had about trifling things, I learned to delight in the truth. I hated being deceived; I had a solid memory; I was gifted with the power of speech; I was softened by the kindness of friends; I rejected pain, crudeness, and ignorance. What wasn't wonderful and praiseworthy about such a state?

But all these are gifts from my God. I didn't give them to myself. They are good in themselves and taken together constitute who I am as a person. So the one who has given them to me is also good, and he is my good, and I thank him for every good he gave me as a boy. My sin was this—that I sought for pleasures, honors, and truth, not in God himself but in creatures, myself and others, and in doing so fell into sorrows, troubles, and mistakes.

Thanks to you, my joy, my pride, my confidence, my God; thanks to you for your gifts. But I pray for you to keep them safe for me. In this way you will keep me safe as well, and those things that you have given me will be developed and perfected.

And I shall be with you, for my very being comes from you.

BOOK 2

Adolescence Lust [2.1–2.3]

1. I now want to go back to recall my past foulness and the bodily sins I engaged in that corrupted my soul—not because I love them, but because I love you, my God. It's because of my love for you that I do this, dredging up my wicked ways in the bit-

terness of remembrance, so that this bitterness may be replaced by your sweetness . . . Let me call to mind those degenerate ways of mine, by which, in turning away from you, I lost myself among a multitude of worldly distractions and fell to pieces. For during my youth, I desired only to be satisfied by worldly things and I became wild in the pursuit of shadowy loves. My beauty wasted away, I stank in your sight, concerned only with pleasing myself and winning favor in the eyes of others.

2. And what was it that delighted me? Nothing other than to love and be loved. But I wasn't measured in my love, and didn't aspire to the kind of union, one mind to another, that one finds in the bright path of friendship. Instead, out of the dark desires of the flesh and the stirrings of puberty, my heart was clouded over until I could no longer distinguish the clear calm of love from the fog of lust. Both boiled over within me and dragged me, young and unstable as I was, over the precipice of my desires, drowning me in a gulf of sins. Your anger had gathered over me, but I didn't realize it. I had grown deaf by the clanking chains of my own mortality, the punishment for my soul's pride. I was wandering further and further away from you, and you let me go. I was tossed about here and there, wasted and dissipated, boiling over in my fornication. And still you remained silent. O my joy, so late in coming! You remained silent while I wandered further from you into the barren lands of my own sorrow, deflated in my arrogance and wearied by my restlessness.

If only there would have been someone around who could have restrained my disorder—someone who might have been able to help transform the fleeting beauties of the things around me into something more useful to me and place boundaries upon their delights. Then if the tides of my youth couldn't have been calmed, they might instead have been cast upon the shores of marriage and used to produce offspring, as your law ordains....

Instead, poor fool that I was, I churned about like the stormy sea. Forsaking you, I followed the turbulent course of my own tide and burst out of all bounds. But I did not escape your punishments, for what mortal can do that? You were always there with me, mercifully angry, making sure that all my illicit pleasures were tainted with bitterness, so that I might seek the sort of pleasures that are free from sorrow. Of course, that could only come through you, Lord . . .

And so, in my sixteenth year, the frenzy of lust... took control over me and I yielded completely to it. All the while, no one in my family made an effort to save me from ruin by arranging for me to get married. Instead, their only concern was that I learned how to speak well and become a persuasive orator.

3. In that year, my education was interrupted. I came back home from Madura, a neighboring city, where I had gone to study grammar and rhetoric. Money was being gathered so that I could study later on at Carthage—my father having more enthusiasm for the idea than ability to pay himself, being a poor citizen of Thagaste . . . At that time, however, he was praised for going well beyond his means to provide his son with the opportunity to study so far away. Many citizens far wealthier than he did no such thing for their children. But my father didn't care at all about how I was growing up in relation to you or how chaste I was. As long as I was sufficiently cultivated, he didn't concern himself with how barren I was to you . . .

This sixteenth year of mine was spent in idleness, due to my family's financial constraints. Not having to do any schoolwork at all while I lived with them, the thorn bushes of lust rose above my head and there was no one to tear them up by the roots. Instead, when my father saw at the baths that I showed signs of becoming a man . . . he gleefully told my mother about it, as though he was already promised grandchildren . . .

Although my father was still relatively new to the faith, you had already started to build your temple in my mother's heart ..
. She warned me with great anxiety . . . not to engage in sexual immorality, and, in particular, to avoid corrupting another man's wife. To me this seemed like the kind of advice women give and I simply ignored it. But these warnings came from you, although I didn't realize it. I thought that you were silent to me and that was just my mother who was speaking to me, when in fact it was you who was speaking to me through her. You were not silent, and in scorning her I was scorning you . . .

But I failed to realize this. Instead I rushed along in my own blindness, and when I heard my friends boasting of their own sexual exploits, I was embarrassed at being more modest than they were. The more shameful their deeds, the more they boasted about them. Even worse, I took pleasure in my own exploits, not just for the pleasure's sake, but mostly for the praise I received . . . Afraid of my friends' contempt, I pretended to have sinned, even when I had not, in order to avoid being thought less courageous for being more innocent than they and less worthy for being more chaste.

With such companions as these I walked the streets of Babylon and wallowed in its filth, as though lounging upon a bed of spices and precious ointments. So that I might stick close to the heart of this city, the invisible enemy trampled upon me and seduced me, for I was eager enough to be seduced. The mother of my flesh already fled from the heart of that city, but still lingered on its outskirts. Although she warned me to preserve my virginity, she didn't . . . take steps to restrain my sexual desires within the bounds of matrimony, if they couldn't be eradicated completely. She didn't take these steps because she was concerned that a wife would prove a hindrance to my hopes—not the hope that she herself had placed in you for the life to come, but the hopes that my parents had entertained for my career. Both my parents were anxious that I succeed in life—my father because he thought next to nothing about you and had only vain thoughts about me; my mother because she thought that the path of traditional education would do me no harm and might actually lead me to you. At least that's my interpretation as I think back upon their intentions.

Meanwhile, the reigns of discipline were loosened upon me. Without any restraints to keep me in order, I was allowed to stray in various disrespectable ways. In all this, there was a heavy mist preventing me from seeing the bright light of your truth, my God . . .

The Pear Theft [2.4–2.6]

4. Your law punishes theft, Lord; so too does the law written in human hearts, which not even sin itself can erase. For what thief would ever submit to being robbed by another thief, even when he is wealthy and the one robbing him is poor. But I wanted to steal and did so, though I was not compelled by any kind of want, but rather through a contempt for goodness and strong impulse towards sinfulness. I already had plenty of what I stole and of a far better quality. Nor did I wish to enjoy what I stole but derived

my joy from the theft itself and the desire to do what was wrong.

Not far from our own vineyard was a pear tree, filled with fruit, although the fruit wasn't particularly enticing in either appearance or flavor. My wretched friends and I went to shake the fruit off the tree and carry it off in the dark of night, after we had finished playing as we usually did in the streets. We took as many pears as we could carry, but not to eat ourselves. Although we may have tasted a few, our real motivation was simply to do what was forbidden.

This was what my heart was like, O God, this was what my heart was like! You had pity on it even when it had sunken to abysmal depths. But now let me confess to you what I was looking for there when I was being so gratuitously wicked, with no other reason for doing wrong than the desire to do wrong itself. The act was loathsome and I loved it! I was in love with my own ruin, in love with my own sin—not the object for which I had sinned, but the sin itself. I was nothing more than a depraved soul, leaping from your firm foundation into my own destruction, seeking nothing from the foul deed, but the foulness itself.

5. There is an attractiveness to material things that draws us to objects like gold and silver, in the sensations involved in the sense of touch, and the reactions of other sensations to their objects. Worldly honor and the power to command and give orders to others have a similar appeal . . . But when it comes seeking these sorts of things, we mustn't depart from you, Lord, or from your law. The life which we have here also has its own enchantments, because it possesses a certain measure of beauty and harmony of a lower sort. And human friendship has a sweetness all its own in bonding one human being to another. Yet sin is committed with all these lower goods when we turn to them with an inordinate desire and neglect the better and higher good—you, our Lord God, your truth, and your law. These things certainly have their delights, but not like my God, who made them all . . .

6. And so what did I, wretch that I was, love in you, this theft of mine, this dark deed committed during my sixteenth year? There was nothing beautiful about you, because you were just theft. But do you even exist at all for me to be speaking to you in this way? Those pears we stole were indeed beautiful, because they were part of your creation, most beautiful of beings, creator of all, good

God, my highest and truest good. The pears were truly beautiful, but it was not for them that my miserable soul lusted. I had far better pears of my own. I stole them simply for the sake of stealing, since afterwards I threw them away. My sole delight was in my own sin; when I put them into my mouth, what sweetened them was my own sin. And so, my Lord God, I ask what so delighted me about my act of theft. There was no beauty in it at all—certainly not the kind of beauty that exists in wisdom or justice, nor in that which is found in the mind, memory, senses, physical vitality. Nor is it the kind of beauty found in the starts, set in the courses, or the earth and sea, teeming with ever newborn life. It even lacked the false, shadowy beauty of deceptive vices . . .

A soul commits fornication when it turns away from you and attempts to find outside you what it is incapable of finding in pure and unadulterated form unless it returns to you. Therefore, those who set themselves apart from you and attempt to lift themselves up against you are trying to perversely imitate you. And yet, even in this imitating of you, they unintentionally acknowledge you as the creator of all things and that there is in fact no place where they can completely separate themselves from you.

What was it then that I loved in this theft of mine? In what sense, Lord, did I attempt to imitate you in my malice and perversity? Did I enjoy violating the law . . . so that I might mimic a shadowy version of your own omnipotence? What a joke! I was like a servant fleeing from his lord and hiding in the shadows. What foulness! What a monstrous life in the depths of death! Could I possibly have found pleasure in what was forbidden simply because it was forbidden? . . .

8. What benefit did I receive from these things which now cause me shame to remember? . . . From a theft that I loved only for theft's sake? The act of theft was nothing and it was for that reason that I, in loving it, was all the more miserable. But if I was alone, I never would have done it . . . I loved the act of theft then because of the companionship of those who with whom I committed it . . .

9. Behold, my God, this vivid remembrance of my soul. By myself, I would never have committed this theft that pleased me so little . . . What an unfriendly sort of friendship it is that leads to an unaccountable seduction of the mind! Out of a hunger for

amusement and mischief came a desire to hurt without any desire on my part for profit or revenge. As soon as others say, "Let's go do it," we become ashamed not to be shameless.

10. Who is there capable of unraveling such a tangled, twisted knot? The act was so revolting that I hate to think about it; I hate to look at it. It is you that I long for, my righteousness and innocence, so beautiful and delightful to the eyes. I longed for you with an insatiable satiety. In you is total peace and freedom from all disturbances. The person who enters into you experiences the joy of his Lord, shall have no fear, and shall find his supreme good in one who is supreme goodness itself.

But in my youth I went astray from you, my God, wandering far from your support. And I became a wasteland to myself.

BOOK 3

The Cauldron of Carthage [3.1 - 3.3]

1. I came to Carthage, where a cauldron of unholy loves sizzled up around me. I wasn't yet in love, but I loved the idea of being in love. Out of a deep sense of hunger, I hated myself for not being even more hungry. In love with the prospect of loving, I was looking for an object of love, but a safe path without snares was repugnant to me. Inside, I was starving for that food that is yourself, my God . . .

My soul was sick and full of sores, and, as it thrust itself outward into worldly things, it sought to comfort itself through contact with objects of the senses. But these physical things were soulless and could not be objects of love. For me, it was sweet to love and be loved—and sweeter still if I could enjoy the body of my lover. I therefore polluted the spring of friendship with the filth of physical desire and clouded its purity with hellish lust. Yet, as foul and immoral as I was, I still desired, in my own extreme vanity, to be through elegant and sophisticated. And so I rushed recklessly into the love for which I longed.

O my God, my mercy, how much bitterness you sprinkled over that sweetness! For, although I was loved and had begun to experience the pleasures of sexual union, I also found myself... bound by chains of misery, and scourged by the red hot iron rods of jealousy, suspicion, fears, angers, and disagreements . . .

3. . . . I consumed myself in sins, fed by a sacrilegious curiosity . . . Once, in your church, while the solemn rites were being celebrated, I even dared to lust after a girl and planned a liaison that merited death. So, you beat me down with heavy punishments, but nothing worse than the pangs of my own conscience. You, my God, were my great mercy and refuge during the terrible dangers I faced. In my pride, I wandered further and further from you, loving my own ways, not yours, delighting in the freedom of a runaway slave.

The studies that I was pursuing at that time were considered highly respectable and were aimed a career in the law courts—a field where the more unscrupulous I was the higher my reputation would be. (The blindness of human beings is so great that they even glory in their blindness.) By this time I had become an advanced student in the school of rhetoric and so proud of this honor that I became swollen up with arrogance. Still, Lord, as you know, I was a relatively quiet student compared to those "subverters," whose perverse nickname was regarded almost as a mark of sophistication among my peers. I caroused with them and enjoyed their friendships, though I abhorred their acts of violence in tormenting . . . younger students for no good reason, solely for their own amusement. Nothing could be described as more like the action of devils than this. "Subverters," therefore, was an apt name for them . . .

Set on Fire:
The Path of Illumination

Confessions 3.4 - 6.5

By the fourth section of Book 3 of the *Confessions,* Augustine has begun to realize that his dissolute way of life could not lead him to the happiness for which he so longed. Like any intelligent person, he begins to explore the various religious and philosophical options available to him at the time. Through God, he will ultimately be led right back to the Catholic faith of his childhood. This is the path of illumination—the opening of the mind to divine truth.

It all begins with a book. While still studying in Carthage, Augustine is given a copy of Cicero's *Hortensius*, which is an exhortation to pursue a philosophical way of life. He is set "on fire" by the work and dedicates himself to the pursuit of the truth through the use of his own reason.[3.4] Cicero also inspires him to pick up the Bible again, but he is immediately turned off by its simplistic style. The problem, he maintains, is that it takes humility to discover the truth in Scripture, and that is precisely what he is lacking.[3.5]

It is at this point in the story that Augustine undergoes his second major conversion—this time to Manichaeism.[3.6-3.9] The Manichaeans were a Christian sect—a fact that certainly appealed to Augustine's desire to stay part of the religion of his childhood. Like Cicero, the Manichaeans preached a form of "heroic humanism" in which one could overcome the temptations of the body by the efforts of one's own will.

Manichaeism was a dualistic religion that intermingled elements of Christianity and Zoroastrianism. The Manicheans believed that there were two primordial forces in the Universe, Light (God, the spiritual) and Dark (the Devil, the material). The force of Light is responsible for the creation of the soul, while the force of Darkness is responsible for the creation of the body. Since human beings contain both elements of light and darkness in them, they are the principle battleground between these two forces.

A good Manichean, seeking to attain salvation, had only to deny the needs of his body, through a rigid form of asceticism. If he succeeded, he would eventually be freed of the "prisons" of his body and the material world and would be able to live a purely spiritual existence in heaven. If he failed, he was condemned to be reborn into another body after death.

For Augustine, Manichaeism offered a neat explanation of the existence of evil in the Universe by attributing it to the work of the force of Darkness (the Devil). It also helped understand the slavery to sin that he experienced without necessarily making him responsible for it, since it was his flesh that was dragging his otherwise good soul into sin.[3.6-3.9]

Naturally, Augustine's pious mother, Monica, was not at all happy about his conversion to Manichaeism. Fortunately, she receives a dream assuring her of Augustine's ultimate conversion back to Catholicism.[3.11] Being a rather persistent woman, she also pesters a local Catholic bishop to set her boy straight. He, however, assures her that Augustine would eventually return to the Church once he realized just how absurd Manichaeism actually is.[3.12]

In Book 4, Augustine recounts how he began to put his education to work, teaching rhetorical skills to young men in Carthage. In 370 he also begins a common-law relationship with a nameless woman, who bears him his only child, Adeodatus, in 372. We know that, although Augustine never married this woman, he was clearly in love with her, since he spent the next 15 years living faithfully with her.[4.2] Of course, in his later years, Augustine will look back on this union with some regret, since he then recognizes that there is a world of difference between a marital covenant blessed by God and even the most committed common-law relationship.

Augustine's relative happiness during this period of his life

is marred by a tragedy that occurs to a close friend of his, whom
he had led into the Manichean faith. This friend is stricken with
a sudden illness and, while he is unconscious, his family has him
baptized in the Catholic faith. Eventually he recovers somewhat
but wants nothing to do with Augustine as long as he remains a
heretic. When his friend finally dies, Augustine is devastated.[4.4]
His grave error, he reflects, was not that he loved his friend, but
that he loved him with the kind of love that should have been re-
served for God alone. In doing so he pollutes this love and turns it
into a form of idolatry.[4.5-4.12]

When he was 29 years old, something happened to Augustine
that led him to become dissatisfied with Manichaeism. One of the
great leaders of the Manichaeans, Faustus of Mileve, had come
to Carthage in 382, and Augustine was hoping that this Faustus,
who was known for being a persuasive speaker, could address
some of his concerns about the religion. Instead, he is disappoint-
ed to discover that Faustus couldn't respond adequately to any
of his problems with the Manichean faith.[5.6] The only positive
thing that Augustine can say about him was that he was modest
enough to recognize his own limitations as a thinker. The result of
his encounter with Faustus is that Augustine gradually begins to
lose interest in Manichaeism, and is resolved to find some better
system to put in its place.[5.7]

The following year (383), Augustine decides to leave Carthage
for Rome. Although this was a serious move for him to make, he
is aided by having Manichean connections in Rome to help him
get established. This is an opportunity for a young man from the
provinces to earn a nice living and perhaps gain a reputation as a
teacher.[5.8]

Through his relations with the Manichaeans, Augustine is later
also given to the opportunity to go to Milan to become a professor of rhetoric. Besides being the capital of the Roman Empire
at this time, Milan is also a city where Christian Neo-Platonism
is spreading like wild-fire. At the heart of this movement is the
Catholic Bishop of the city, Ambrose. Augustine is immediately
swept off his feet by Ambrose's sermons, which combined a delightful rhetorical style with far more intelligent doctrine than he
had ever heard from the Manichaeans. Augustine begins to realize that, despite Manichean objections, the Catholic faith, in fact,

makes a good deal of sense. [5.13-14]

Ambrose shows Augustine that the Old Testament (which the Manichaeans rejected) could be read figuratively and was in complete accord with the New Testament. Later Augustine will also be shown how to think about God and the soul in purely spiritual terms when he discovers the famed "books of the Platonists." With the help of Ambrose, he finally has the courage to reject Manichaeism and become a catechumen in the Catholic Church. Although he is still not a committed Catholic, he has run out of viable options.[5.14]

In Book 6, the process of illumination continues as Augustine becomes more actively involved in the Catholic community of Milan. Although Augustine doesn't have the opportunity to ask Ambrose specific questions about the Catholic faith, he is learning quite a bit just by listening to the Bishop's sermons on Sunday. Specifically, he is now on the path to developing a truly spiritual understanding of God and the soul, as opposed to his prior crude Manichean materialism.[6.3] He also begins to realize that those teachings from Scripture which used to be absurd to him now make perfect sense when interpreted in allegorical rather than a literal manner.[6.4]

Now that Augustine's objections to the Catholic faith have all been eliminated, he begins to see that Catholicism is far preferable to all the other approaches—secular philosophy and Manichaeism in particular—that he had previously toyed with. What impresses him the most about the Catholicism that he encounters in Milan is that it demands belief in a higher truth that cannot be rationally demonstrated. Also, whereas Manichaeism and secular philosophy are fit only for an intellectual elite, the truths of the Catholic faith are accessible both to the simplest believer as well as to the most profound thinker.[6.5]

Related Readings

Augustine. "Plundering the Gold of the Egyptians"
Augustine. "The Goodness of Creation"

BOOK 3

"Coming Upon" Philosophy [3.4 - 3.5]

4. . . . At a very vulnerable time of my life, I began to study text-books on eloquence. I wanted to become eminent in this field out of a damnable and conceited desire to appease my human vanity. In the normal course of my studies, I came upon a certain book by Cicero, a man whose language is universally admired, though not his heart. This particular book of his, called *Hortensius*, contains an exhortation to study philosophy. Now it was this book that changed my whole attitude and turned my prayers to you, O Lord, for it gave me new hopes and desires. At once, all of my vain hopes became worthless to me, and, with an incredible warmth of heart, I began to desire the immortality of wisdom. I began now to rise up in order to return to you. It was not to sharpen my way of speaking that I read the book (though this was supposed to be the purpose of my studies that I pursued in my nineteenth year, paid for by my mother, since my father had died two years earlier). What inspired me about [this book] was not its style but its contents.

My God, how I burned to fly from earthly things to you! I didn't know at that time what you were trying to do with me. In Greek, the love of wisdom is called "philosophy," and this book inflamed my love for it. There are some who use philosophy to lead us astray, coloring and disguising their own errors by using that great, wonderful, and honorable name. Nearly all who did so in Cicero's time and before are noted and criticized in that book....

At that time . . . I was so delighted by this exhortation to wisdom that I was aroused, kindled, and set on fire to love, seek, acquire, and hold, not the ideas of this or that sect, but wisdom itself, wherever it was to be found. There was only one thing that held me back in my great enthusiasm: that the name of Christ was not mentioned in the book . . . And any book in which this name was missing—no matter how well-written, elegant, or true it may have been—could ever entirely captivate me.

5. I therefore decided to turn my attention to the holy scriptures to see what they were like. But here I saw something that

could not be understood by the proud, nor laid open to children. Here was something simplistic at first glance, but far loftier as one penetrates its depths—something veiled in mystery. I, however, was not yet able to enter into it or to bow my head to follow its pathways. I felt differently then than I do now: for when I studied the scriptures, I felt that they were unworthy in comparison to the grand style of Cicero. My inflated pride shrank from their lowliness and my intelligence failed to perceive their meaning. These scriptures would aid the growth of a little child, but I hated the thought of being childlike. In my great pride, I fancied myself all grown up.

Conversion to Manichaeism [3.6 - 3.10]

6. And so I fell into companionship with a group of men who were mad with pride, completely carnal, and endless prattling, in whose mouths were the snares of the devil . . . They would repeatedly cry out, "Truth! Truth!" and they were forever telling me about it. But there was never any truth in what they said, since they told me lies not only about you, who are Truth, but also about the nature of the world, your creation. And, indeed, I should have gone beyond the philosophers who spoke the truth about these things out of my love for you, my father, my highest good and beauty of all things beautiful.

Truth! Truth! How I panted after you, even in the deepest marrow of my soul, even as these Manichaeans frequently and in various ways called out your name—though it was a mere sound. In the dishes they served up to meet my hunger, they laid out the sun, the moon, and all your beautiful creations, but not you yourself or even your primary works. For your spiritual works are far greater than these material works, celestial and glittering though they may be. But I was hungry and thirsty, not even for these first works of yours, but for you yourself, the truth, in whom there is no variability . . .

7. I was being persuaded to agree with those foolish deceivers by the questions they were constantly asking me: What is the origin of evil? Was God bound by material form and has he hair and nails? Should we consider righteous those who had many wives, killed human beings and made animal sacrifices? In my

ignorance, I was greatly disturbed by these questions and while I was retreating from the truth, I had the impression that I was going towards it. I didn't yet understand that evil was nothing but a privation of the good—that, in fact, it has no being. And how could I have understood this when my sight was limited to physical bodies and my mind to fantasies. I did not know that God is a spirit, not a thing with parts extended in length and breadth, nor the kind of being having a particular size. And I was entirely ignorant of what it was in us that gives us existence and which is said in Scripture to be made in God's image . . .

10. I was ignorant of these things and so mocked those holy servants and prophets of yours. And yet what did I gain by mocking them, except to be mocked by you in turn. Gradually and unconsciously, I was lured into such absurdities as believing that a fig weeps when it is plucked, and its mother tree too weeps milky tears. But if a Manichaean saint ate such a fig—provided that the sin of picking it was done by someone else's hand and not his—he would digest it and breathe out angels, or even particles of God. These particles of the most high and true God would have remained trapped in the fruit if not set free by the chewing and digestion of one of the elect "saints." And I, poor fool that I was, believed that more mercy should be shown to the fruits of the earth than to my fellow human beings, for whom these fruits were created. For if a hungry person, who was not a Manichaean, asked for a bit of this food and it were given, that morsel would have been considered as condemned to capital punishment.

A Hint of Things to Come [3.11 - 3.12]

11. And now you stretched forth your hand from above, drawing my soul out of that deep darkness. Your faithful servant, my mother, was weeping for me to you—more bitterly than even mothers mourn the bodily deaths of their children. By that faith and spirit which she had from you, she recognized the death that held me, and you, Lord, heard her. You didn't despise the tears, streaming down, when they watered the ground underneath her eyes every place that she prayed. Indeed, you heard her.

How else could one explain that dream of hers, by which you so comforted her, which resulted in her allowing me to live with her and eat at the same table in her house. She originally had refused me, horrified by my blasphemous errors. But she had a dream in which she saw herself standing on a kind of wooden ruler. A young beautiful man with radiant face came to her. He smiled at her, though she was sorrowful and overcome with grief. He asked her the reason for her grief and daily tears—though the point of the question, as usual in such visions, was to teach her, not to elicit information from her. She replied that she mourned my ruin. He told her to have no fear and directed her to look and see that where she was, I was also. When she looked, she saw me standing beside her on the same ruler.

How else could this vision have come about, unless your ears were open to her heart. O you good, all-powerful, God: you care for each one of us as if we were yours alone and for all as if they were but one.

And how could it be explained that, when she related this vision to me, I tried to bend it to mean that she could not give up hope of one day becoming what I was. But she promptly replied without any hesitation, "No, I was not told, 'Where he is, you will be too' but 'where you are, he will be.'"

I confess to you, Lord, that to the best of my memory—and I have often spoken of this incident—I was more deeply disturbed by this answer that came from you from my watchful mother than by the dream itself. She was not at all perplexed by the plausibility of my false interpretation, but immediately saw the truth, as I had not until she spoke. That dream foretold the future joy in store for this devout woman as a consolation for her present sorrows. For almost nine years passed in which I wallowed in the deep mire and the darkness of falsehood, often trying to free myself, only to be plunged back again. Yet, throughout these years, this chaste, holy, and sensible widow, of a kind you so dearly love, though she now had more hope for me, never ceased her weeping and mourning about me to you. Though you heard her pleas, still you allowed me to tumble and toss in the darkness.

12. Meanwhile you gave my mother another answer, as I recall. I'm passing over much now, because I feel compelled to focus on those things that made me want to confess to you, and there is a great deal I simply don't remember. You gave her another answer through a priest of yours, a certain Bishop raised in your Church

and well-trained in your scriptures. My mother begged this bishop to make time to talk to me, to refute my errors, and to teach me what was correct, for he used to do this whenever he found someone worthy of instruction. But he refused—wisely, as I later understood. He responded that I was not yet ready to be taught, still being arrogantly enchanted with the novelty of that heresy, and because, as she had informed him, I had corrupted the minds of many untrained persons with my petty questions. "Leave him alone," he said, "Just pray to the Lord for him, and he'll discover his errors for himself by reading and how great his impiety is." During the same conversation, he informed her how he himself, as a young child, had been handed over to the Manichaeans by his deluded mother. Not only had he read all their books but had even written some himself. Without anyone arguing with him or attempting to convince him of his errors, it had become clear to him that this sect ought to be fled from. And so he left it.

But, even upon hearing this, my mother still refused to be satisfied. She urged him even more with begging and tears to see me and set me straight. Eventually, the Bishop, somewhat annoyed with her, said, "Go away now and let me be. As you live, it can certainly not be that the son of these tears should perish." In later conversations with me, she would often recall that she had taken these words as if they came from heaven itself.

BOOK 4

Career and Family in Carthage [4.1 - 4.2]

1. During that nine-year period—from my nineteenth to my twenty-eighth year—I lived a life of seducing and being seduced, deceiving and being deceived, always subject to a multitude of desires. Publicly, I was a teacher of the so-called liberal arts; privately I practiced a false religion. In the former role I was arrogant, in the latter superstitious, and in both vain . . .

2. During those years, I taught the art of rhetoric, and in my greed sold the gift of speech whereby one could overcome others. Nevertheless, Lord, as you know, I preferred having virtuous students—or at least those who could pass for virtuous. Without any tricks on my part, I taught the art of trickery, not so that they

should be used to take the life of an innocent man, but that sometimes they might be used to save the life of a guilty one . . .

At this time I also lived with a woman—not one bound to me
in lawful marriage, but who I discovered in my misguided and ignorant passion. But she was my only woman and I remained sex-
ually faithful to her. Through this experience I learned first-hand
how great a difference there is between proper marriage entered
into for the sake of having children and an agreement entered into
through lustful desires in which children may be born against the
parents' wishes—though once they are born the parents feel compelled to love them.

The Death of His Friend in Thagaste [4.4 - 4.13]

4. During the time when I first began to teach rhetoric in my native town, I had a friend who became close to me because of our
shared interests. We were both the same age and he was also beginning to flower into manhood. We had grown up together, had
gone to school together and had played together. But he wasn't
the friend at that point that he would become later on, and even
then he wasn't a true friend. For there can be no true friendship
unless those who cling to one another are glued together by you
by that love which is poured into our hearts by the Holy Spirit.

In any event, it was an excessively sweet friendship, developed in an enthusiasm for the studies that we shared together—
excessively sweet, because I turned him away from the true faith,
which he held, because of his youth, in an immature and shal-
low way. I turned him towards those superstitious and dangerous
fairytales that were the source of all my mother's tears for me. I
led him astray with me and I couldn't bear to be without him.

But you were there pursuing close behind us, O God of ven-
geance and fountain of mercy, who turns us back towards you by
wonderous ways. You were there and you took him from this life
after less than a year of friendship—a friendship that was sweeter
to me than any other sweetness I had known in life . . .

Suffering from fever, he lay for a long time unconscious and
in a death sweat. When his condition was thought to be critical,
he was baptized without his knowledge. I ignored this, because
I believed that he would remember what I had taught him and

would not be affected by what had been done to his body while he was unconscious. But it turned out quite differently. He eventually recovered and was restored to health. As soon as I could speak to him—which I was able to do as soon as he could speak to me, since I never left his side and we were deeply attached to one another—I tried to joke about the baptism that he had received when he was out of his senses and unaware, assuming that he would join in. But he had already learned that he had received the sacrament and turned away from me as though I was his enemy. With an amazing and newfound frankness, he warned me to stop saying such things, if I wanted to remain his friend. I was shocked and troubled. But I put off telling him about my feelings, thinking that once he got better, I could deal with him any way I liked. But he was snatched away from my insane plans to be kept safe with you for my consolation. A few days later, while I was away, his fever returned, and he died.

Grief darkened my heart and, wherever I looked, there was only death. My native land was a torment to me and my father's house a strange misery. Now that he was gone, all those things that we had done together turned into cruel agony without him. My eyes searched for him everywhere, but he was nowhere to be found. I hated everything because he was not there, nor could people tell me now, "look, he's on his way," as used to be the case when he was alive and away from me. I had become a great riddle to myself. I would ask my soul, "Why are you so sad and distressed?" But my soul didn't know the right answer to give....

6. I was unhappy, but so is every soul ensnared by love with things bound to die. It is torn apart by their loss and becomes aware of its unhappiness even before it has lost them. This was how it was with me at this time, and I cried very bitterly and rested in my bitterness. As miserable as I was, my attachment to this life was greater to me than the friend that I had lost . . . I found myself tired of living but terrified of dying. The fact was that the more I loved my friend, the more I believe I hated death, which had taken him from me. I hated it as a cruel and fearful enemy and thought that since it had taken him from me, it was going to consume all human beings. Yes, that was my state of mind as I recall it . . .

7. What madness it is not to know how to love human beings

as they ought to be loved! How ridiculous human beings are to be unable to understand their human predicament! That was my state at the time. So I raged, sighed, wept, and worried. There was no rest for me and no capacity for reason . . . I had become to myself a place of misery, where I could not bear to be but from which I could not escape. For my heart could not escape from my heart, nor could I escape from myself, since, wherever I fled, I would be following. Yet, I did flee from my native land, for my eyes sought him out less in places where they had not seen him before. So I left Thagaste and came to Carthage.

8. Time does not stand still, nor does it idly slip through our senses. Its passing has wonderous effects on the mind. So now time came and went from day to day and by its passing implanted within me other things to hope for and remember. Bit by bit, it healed me through old kinds of pleasure, allowing my sorrow to give way. But these delights, though they didn't bring me new sorrows, brought the seeds of new sorrows. For the reason that sorrow had been so easily and deeply able to pierce me was because I had poured out my soul, like water onto sand, by loving a man bound to die as though he were an immortal. What restored and repaired me was the company of other friends who I loved. In loving them, I was loving what was a substitute for you . . .

[But] blessed is he who loves you, and loves his friends in you, and loves his enemies because of you. He alone loses no one dear to him, for all are dear to him who can't be lost. And who is this except our God . . . ? No one loses you unless he leaves you. And if he leaves you, where can he go, where can he escape? He can only run from your kindness to your anger. Doesn't he encounter your law everywhere as his own punishment? For, your law is truth and truth is you . . .

BOOK 5

Dissatisfaction with Manichaeism [5.3 - 5.7]

3. In the sight of God, I will now talk openly about my twenty-eighth year of life. At that time, there had come to Carthage a certain Manichean bishop by the name of Faustus. He was a great trap of the Devil and many were ensnared by the smoothness of

his language. While I too was ready to admire his eloquence, I soon came to distinguish between it and the truth I was eager to learn. What interested me was not how elaborate the dish he served in his speech, but rather the substance of the knowledge he put before me to eat. For I had been informed that he really was a remarkable scholar, particularly in the liberal arts.

Now I had read quite a lot of philosophy, committing a good bit to memory and still retained it. And so, I began to compare certain teachings from my readings to the fables of the Manichaeans. The philosophers' teachings seemed more probable, since these men were able to investigate the world with understanding, even if they were not as successful in discovering its Lord . . .

6. For nine years or so—a period in which, in my intellectual confusion, I remained a hearer in this sect—I waited with intense longing for this Faustus fellow. Other Manichaeans, who I had a chance to meet, were unable to answer my questions. But they kept promising me that when this man arrived and I had the opportunity to discuss matters with him, all these questions of mine, and even greater difficulties, would be sorted through and resolved. When he came, I found him an agreeable, well-spoken man. He said the same sorts of things as the rest, but did so much more elegantly . . . But a good speaking style doesn't make something true, nor is a person wise just because he has a handsome face and uses well-chosen words. Those who had promised so much to me weren't such good judges: to them, this man seemed wise and prudent simply because the way he spoke pleased them . . .

I had waited for the man for quite a long time. My enthusiastic feelings were certainly gratified by his liveliness and expressiveness in debate and when I saw how readily words came to him, as a kind of clothing for his thought. Yes, I definitely was delighted. Along with so many people—and perhaps even more than most—I raved about him. But I was also annoyed that, as part of a large audience I was not allowed to question him or to get answers to the questions bothering me in more intimate conversation and discussion. [When I eventually was able . . .] to raise some of the questions concerning me, I found the man to be rather poorly educated in the liberal arts, with the exception of literature, and his knowledge of even that subject was mediocre at best . . . When I raised my questions with him, he quite modestly and sensibly refused to take up the burden. He knew that he was uninformed in these matters and was not ashamed to admit it. He certainly wasn't like some of the loudmouths who had tried to teach me and had nothing to say . . .

7. As a result of this, I lost all the enthusiasm I had for the [Manichaeans]. I had little hope for any of the other teachers of this sect, now that this man, with his great reputation, had turned out to be so ignorant in all the matters that concerned me. I did however spend a great deal of time with him, because of his great love for literature—a subject that I, as a master of rhetoric, was teaching young men at Carthage . . . But any ideas I had about advancing in the sect were abandoned once I had gotten to know this man. I didn't cut myself off entirely, though. Since I had not yet found anything more satisfactory than this sect that I had blundered into, I decided to stick with it for the time being, until some better option presented itself . . .

Move to Rome [5.8 – 5.9]

8. You acted upon me in such a way that I was persuaded to go to Rome to teach there what I had been teaching in Carthage. I won't omit the means by which you persuaded me, since this reveals the depths of your mystery and your ever-present mercy, which must always be reflected upon and proclaimed.

My motive for going to Rome was not the higher earning potential or greater prestige promised by friends who urged me to go there—though at the time such considerations did have a hold upon me. The more compelling reason for the move, and perhaps the sole one, was that I had heard that the young men there were more serious in their studies and were bound by stricter discipline. They weren't permitted, for instance, to come rushing into the classroom of one who wasn't their own instructor; in fact, they were not allowed to enroll at all without his permission.

At Carthage, on the other hand, the students are disgusting in their wildness. Like madmen they force their way into classrooms and disrupt the discipline that each teacher has established to ensure student success . . . As a student myself, I had always avoided this kind of behavior, but now as a teacher I was forced to endure it. So, I decided to go to Rome where informed people told me that such things didn't happen. But it was you, my hope and share in the land of the living, who wanted me to change my country for the sake of my soul. At Carthage, you provided the sharp thorns to dislodge me from that place, and in Rome you provided enticements that would draw me there . . .

You, God, knew why I needed to leave Carthage for Rome, but you didn't reveal this to me or to my mother, who was terribly distressed by my departure and followed me all the way to the sea. She held on to me with all her strength, determined either to take me back home or come along with me. But I deceived her, pretending that I had a friend I didn't want to leave until the wind was right for him to set sail. I lied to my mother—to such a mother!—and gave her the slip. But you forgave me even this, mercifully saving me in my despicable filth from the waters of the sea until I reached the baptizing water of your grace. Those waters would wash me clean and dry the rivers that flowed from my mother's eyes, by which she watered the ground through her daily prayers for me.

Still, she refused to return home without me, and I was barely able to persuade her to stay that night in a shrine dedicated to the memory of St. Cyprian. During the night, I secretly set out, leaving her behind, praying and weeping. Through that flood of tears, she was begging you not to allow me to sail . . . But you ignored all that. You were using the force of my own greedy desires to put an end to those desires, and you were punishing her with the whip of sorrows for her all too worldly affection for me . . . And yet after she had finished accusing me of deception and cruelty, she went right back to praying for me. She returned home, while I went on to Rome.

9. No sooner had I gotten to Rome, though, when I was attacked by a physical illness that nearly sent me to hell with all the sins I had committed against you, myself, and others—sins so numerous and grave, sins over and above that original sin by which all of us die in the person of Adam. You hadn't forgiven me for any of these yet in Christ, for, by his cross, he had not eliminated any of the sins that I had committed against you. How could he do so when he was crucified as a mere phantom for me, which is how I thought of him? . . .

Although my mother didn't know about any of this, she continued to pray for me. She was far away, but you are present everywhere. Where she was, you heard her; where I was, you had mercy on me. And so, I recovered my bodily health, though I remained sick in my heretical heart. Though in grave danger, I still had no desire for your baptism . . . So, you healed my illness and restored your handmaid's son, preserving me so that you might give me a better and surer health later on.

Even then, during this period when I was in Rome, I continued to associate with those deluded and deceiving "holy ones." I associated not only with the "hearers"—one of whom included the man in whose house I had become sick and was recovering—but also those whom they call "the elect." For I still believed that it was not we who sin, but some other nature within us. It satisfied my pride to think that I was blameless, and, when I had done something wrong, it pleased me not to have to confess to you—a confession that would have healed this soul of mine that had sinned against you. Rather, I preferred to excuse myself and lay the blame at some other force that was within me but not "me". But in fact, I was wholly me and what divided me against myself was my own unholiness. And my sin was all the more incurable due to the fact that I didn't think of myself as a sinner. In my wickedness, I preferred to believe that you, Almighty God, should be defeated within me, rather than to admit that, to be saved, I needed to surrender to you . . .

And so I continued to associate with their elect, even though I had given up hope of advancing any further in their doctrine. I held on to their teachings half-heartedly and without conviction, because I had decided to be content with what I had in the absence of anything preferable . . .

12. I now set myself to the task of teaching rhetoric in Rome—the reason why I had come here in the first place. The first thing I did was gather students to my home, and, with them and through them, I began to gain a reputation. But I soon discovered that things went on in Rome that I hadn't had to put up with in Africa. It was true that none of the acts of subversion by wild young men occurred in Rome. But I was told that instead, to avoid paying their teacher tuition, students conspire together and suddenly go off to study with another teacher. They forsake their pledge and show that justice is cheap to them compared to their love of mon-

ey. I hated them, but not with a perfect hatred; I probably felt more resentment for what they were doing personally to me than because of their general behavior.

Certainly people of this type are shameful characters and break faith with you by fixing their hearts on passing playthings . . . They embrace a world that is fleeting, while despising you who endure forever, who calls them back to you, and who forgives the adulterous heart when it returns to you. I still despise crooked and wicked people of this sort, although I now treat them as individuals to be corrected . . . But back then, when I was threated with harm from these students, I was more concerned with avoiding their evil for my own sake than I was desirous that they become good because of you.

Encountering Catholicism in Milan [5.13 – 5.14]

13. A message had been sent from Milan to Rome to the city prefect to provide them with a professor of rhetoric, and, as an added bonus, his travel was to be provided through government funds. So I decided to apply for this post myself with the assistance of those drunk on the Manichaean faith. My move there would enable me to be rid of these people—though neither I nor they realized that at the time. I had the opportunity to give a sample speech, which was approved by the prefect Symmachus, and I was sent to Milan.

In this way, I came to Milan and to Bishop Ambrose, who was regarded throughout the world as among the best of men—one who ministered to your people through his eloquent sermons . . . I was led to him unknowingly through you so that I might be led knowingly through him to you. That man of God welcomed me with fatherly kindness, and, in his capacity as a bishop, approved of my coming. I began to love him, not at first as a teacher of the truth, since I had no confidence in your church, but simply as a man who was kind to me.

I used to listen eagerly when he preached to the people, but not with the intention I should have had: I wanted to assess whether his eloquence matched its reputation and whether his speaking style was better or worse than it was reported to be. I hung on his words with great attention, but wasn't very interested in their content, which I held in contempt. I was delighted by the charm of his style—more learned, was much less warm and witty than that of Faustus. In content, however, there was no comparison. Faustus simply rambled off Manichaean deceits, while Ambrose taught the wholesome message of salvation. But, for sinners of the kind that I was at the time, salvation is very far off.

Yet, little by little, though I didn't realize it, I was drawing closer.

14. I wasn't really all that interested in learning about what he was saying, but only in how he said it. This was all that was left to me after I had begun despairing that I was ever going to find a way to you. But, as his words, which I admired, began seeping into my mind, the substance of his thought, which I had previously disregarded, began seeping into it as well. For I couldn't separate the one from the other. And so, as I opened my heart to how eloquently he was speaking, I also began to become aware, little by little, of how truthfully he spoke. While I had previously thought that nothing could be said in defense of the Catholic faith in light of Manichaean attacks, it now seemed to me that this faith could be supported quite reasonably . . .

And so I decided that I had to leave the Manichaeans, since, in this period of uncertainty, I didn't think it right to continue as a member of this sect . . . For the time being, I chose to live as a catechumen in the Catholic Church, which was what my parents wanted for me, until I could see by some clear light the path by which I might direct my course.

BOOK 6

The Return of Monica [6.1]

1. Hope of my youth, where were you when I sought you? How had you gone so far away from me? Wasn't it you who made me, and made me superior to the animals on land and wiser than the birds in the air? I was walking along dark and slippery paths. I was looking for you outside myself and failed to find the God of my heart. I had plummeted to the depths of the sea and lost hope that I would ever discover the truth.

My mother had by this time rejoined me. She was so strong in her faith that she didn't hesitate to follow me over land and sea, confident in you, despite all the dangers she faced. In fact, it was she who reassured the sailors during the perils of her sea voyage, although it is typically the sailors who try to give confidence to inexperienced travelers on the high seas. She promised them a safe arrival, because you promised this to her in a vision.

My mother found me in a state of grave despair, having lost all confidence in discovering the truth. When I told her that I was no longer a Manichaean, though not a Catholic Christian either, she didn't leap for joy, as though she had heard something unexpected. She was already confident about my state at this point. She wept for me as a dead man, but one who could still be raised back to life by you . . . She was certain that you, who had promised her everything, would give her what remained. With a tranquil and confident heart, she told me that she had faith that Christ would see me a true Catholic before she died . . .

With great zeal she would rush to the church and listen with rapt attention to Ambrose, whose words she found to be a fountain of water springing up to eternal life. She was devoted to the man as an angel of God and recognized that it was thanks to his efforts that I had been brought to my present place of doubtful wavering. And she foresaw that I would pass from sickness to health, though not without experiencing an even more dangerous state—the crisis period, as physicians call it . . .

The Example of Bishop Ambrose [6.3 - 6.5]

3. I was not yet groaning in prayer for your help, but my mind was keen on inquiry restlessly searching for an argument. I regarded Ambrose himself as a fortunate man by the standards of this world, because so many powerful people respected him. His celibacy was the only thing about him that seemed a hardship. I had no experience of a life like his to guess what hopes he cherished, what struggles against temptation he fought, what consolations he received in adversity, what was in his heart, or what joys he received while chewing on the bread of your world.

For his part, he didn't know the depths of my spiritual turmoil or the deep pit of danger threatening me. I couldn't ask him the questions I had as completely as I wanted to, because of the crowds of people bringing him business and to whose weaknesses he tended. In the little time he had when he was not with them, he was restoring his body with food and his mind with reading. When reading, his eyes scanned the page and his heart unveiled the sense of the text, but his voice and tongue were silent.

We were often with him, since he didn't forbid anyone access to him nor even require that visitors be announced. On these occasions, we would see him reading silently and doing little else. And we would also sit there in silence—for who would dare to interrupt him while he was so engrossed—and then leave quietly. We guessed that, during the small period of time he had to refresh his mind, he wouldn't want to be bothered with other people's problems . . . Another reason for his silence was that he needed to preserve his voice, which was prone to hoarseness. But whatever his reason for acting in this way, it was undoubtedly a good one.

In any case, no opportunity presented itself for me to interrogate [him], except when there was a matter requiring only a brief meeting. The inner turmoil that I was experiencing, however, required a much longer period for me to share my issues with him, but that could never be found.

Nevertheless, I did hear him rightly preaching the truth of the scriptures to the people every Sunday. As I listened to him, I became more and more convinced that the knotty difficulties and twisted lies that those Manichaean deceivers of ours had fashioned could be unraveled. I began to understand that . . . the truth of your creating human beings in your own image shouldn't be understood to suggest by your sons in the spirit that you were limited by the form of a human body. Although I didn't have a clue about what a spiritual substance could be like, yet I blushed in shameful joy at the thought that for so many years I had been yapping, not at the Catholic faith itself, but against figments of my own carnal imaginations . . .

Spiritual Illumination [6.4 - 6.5]

4. Since I didn't know how this image of yours could exist in us, I should have knocked at the door and inquired about the meaning of this doctrine, rather than opposing and insulting it, as if it meant what I thought. My anxiety to discover what I could hold

for certain gnawed at my innermost self and was felt all the more intensely from the shame I felt at having suffered so long from a delusion . . .

And so I was greatly embarrassed and did an about-face. I rejoiced to find that your one Church, the body of your only son . . . didn't hold to infantile fallacies: she didn't, in her sound doctrine, maintain that you, creator of all things, occupy some physical space, that, vast and broad as it may be, nevertheless was confined on all sides in the same manner as human bodies.

I was also pleased that the ancient writings of the law and the prophets were no longer being presented to me for reading in a way that had made them look absurd before, when I used to attack your followers for holding views that they clearly didn't hold at all. And I was delighted whenever I heard Ambrose proclaim frequently to his congregation the following basic principle—that "the letter kills, but the spirit gives life." In this way he would unveil the hidden mystery and opened up to his listeners the deeper meaning of the passage, which, if taken literally, would seem wrong. I couldn't object to anything that he said, even though I wasn't yet certain whether what he said was true or not. . . . For I wanted to be as certain about the things I couldn't see as I was that seven plus three makes ten . . .

I could have been healed by believing, so that my mind's eye, thus purified, would have been directed towards your truth, which is eternal and unfailing. But, as commonly happens, I was like someone who has suffered at the hands of a bad physician and afraid to entrust myself to a good one. So it was with the care of my soul. I could have been cured by believing, but I feared believing something false . . .

5. From this time on, however, I began to prefer the Catholic faith. In requiring belief in what couldn't be proven...I thought the Church showed greater modesty and more honesty than the Manichaeans who rashly promised certain knowledge and mocked faith, but then demanded belief in a whole host of fabulously absurd myths that certainly couldn't be demonstrated.

Then, little by little, Lord, you began working to calm my heart with your gentle and merciful hand. I began to see that there were countless things that I believed without seeing or being present when they happened—for example, numerous historical events or facts about places and cities I had never visited. And there are also those many things I believed based upon the word of friends, physicians, and various other people. These were things we had to accept, or we simply couldn't function in life. I also considered how solid was my certainty that I had been born of particular parents, a fact that I could not know without believing the word of others.

And so, you convinced me that the truly blameworthy people were not the ones who believed in these books of yours, which you established with great authority as a foundation for all nations, but those who didn't believe in them. Nor were they to be listened to who challenged me by asking, "How do you know that these books were provided to the human race by the spirit of the one, true, and most truthful God?"

This, then, was the thing I most needed to believe, because none of the slanderous questions that I had read in the works of those ever-squabbling philosophers could shake the belief from me that you exist (though I couldn't determine what your exact nature was) and that you direct the course of human affairs. This belief was sometimes stronger in me and sometimes weaker. But I always believed that you existed and took care of us, even if I didn't know what to believe about your essential nature or what way would lead me to, or back to, you.

It was because we were too feeble to discover the truth through pure reason that we needed the authority of sacred scripture. I now began to understand that there was no way that you could have conferred such supreme authority to these scriptures—now spread throughout all lands—unless you saw them as a means whereby men would both come to believe in you and seek to know you.

Having now heard many plausible explanations for passages in these books that had formerly struck me as absurd, I now came to understand the depth of their profound mysteries. In fact, the authority of the scriptures seemed all the more worthy of veneration and faith, because, while it was easy for everyone to read, it also allowed more subtle thinkers to plumb the depths of its hidden mysteries. In plain words and a simple style, it offered itself to everybody, but also forced serious thinkers to exert themselves. Thus its arms were wide open to receive everyone, but it also drew a few in through its narrow ways . . .

As I reflected on these things, Lord, you stood by me. I sighed, and you heard me. I was tossed about, and you steadied me. I traveled along the broad paths of this world, but you didn't abandon me.

The Will at War with Itself:
The Path of Purgation

Confessions 6.6 - 8.12

H aving begun to recognize the truth of the Catholic faith, Augustine now finds himself at another stumbling point with respect to his never-ending quest to find happiness in life. Though he knows intellectually the right way to live his life in order to be saved, he finds that he lacks the will to act as he desires. The next stage in his spiritual development has to be the purification of his will, leading to his own moral conversion.

In *Confessions* 6.6 he makes an analogy between himself and a poor drunken beggar that is meant to illustrate for the reader the futility of Augustine's own quest for the happy life. The beggar deludes himself into thinking that his drunken revelries make him happy; Augustine deludes himself into thinking that his own quest for fame will make him happy. Both are equally foolish, but at least the beggar gets a few moments reprieve from his cares. The two actually suffer from the same "disease"—disordered love or lust. The beggar's lust is for drink, Augustine's for fame and glory. Both crave some limited good in an absolute way and are enslaved by their disordered longing. Neither, therefore, is able to find the happiness he seeks.

It is at this point in the Confessions that Augustine seems to digress from his own story to talk about a few incidents in the life of his friend, Alypius. Actually, Augustine uses this story as a means of illustrating the mysterious working of Providence in the lives of those around him. The same pattern of conversion that we will see in this story as well as that of Victorinus in Book 8, we will also see in Augustine's own conversion story.

The end result of these accounts is the same: the individual involved is inflamed with such a delight in God that all of his previous love interests seem pale in comparison. The passive language used in all these accounts, and the immediacy of conversion after a long period of personal struggle with habitual behavior similarly point to divine rather than human activity at work .

Augustine has now reached the age of 30, and although he recognizes the truth of the Catholic faith, he still is incapable of taking those steps necessary to reform his life. Although he knows that he should give up his vain ambitions (for career, status, wealth, marriage), he lacks the resolve to carry out his good intentions. He also finds himself still tempted by the need for sexual intimacy and believes that he lacks the power to ever reform himself. His mistake, however, is precisely to believe that he has to do all this on his own. All he really needs to do is to ask God for help and he will be cured. What he lacks at this point is the humility to do this.[6.11]

He still is contemplating the prospects of an "honorable marriage," but actually wants to get married for the wrong reason—that is, simply to provide an outlet for his sexual longing. His mother, to keep him on the right path, arranges a marriage between him and a younger woman from a respectable family. Because she is under-aged, he has to wait two years until he can marry her.[6.12-13] These plans for marriage interfere with Augustine's attempt to found a lay religious community with his friends in Milan, because they couldn't figure out what to do with their wives.[6.14]

While Augustine is engaged to be married, he realizes that he must separate from his common-law wife. (Although mistresses were tolerated among pagans, they were certainly frowned upon in Christian circles.) She is sent back to Africa, and his pain at their separation is evidence that he loved her deeply. He is such a slave to his passions, however, that he finds another sexual partner to satisfy his lust.[6.15]

At the beginning of Book 7, Augustine still is having problems being able to conceive of God in an intelligible way, since he continues to conceive of the divine being as a "corporeal substance" (i.e., a material being). He certainly cannot even begin to understand how anything can exist outside of space and time.[7.1]

At least he no longer is caught up in his previous Manichean errors about God. He recognizes that if there are two primordial substances in the universe continually at war with one another (Good and Evil, God and the Devil), then either God cannot eliminate the force of darkness (in which case he is not omnipotent) or he simply chooses not to do so (in which case he is not supremely good).[7.2] This leaves Augustine to speculate about the cause of evil in the universe. The cause can certainly not be God, who is supremely good and has created only good things. He then concludes that the cause of evil is nothing other than the free will of human beings used for evil purposes. However, at times it seemed to Augustine that he often did wicked things seemingly against his own will. How can we account for that? The answer is that this inability to do the good he wills is nothing other than a penalty for sins that he freely committed.[7.3 - 7.4]

In *Confessions* 7 we arrive at one of the most important passages in the Confessions: Augustine's encounter with the books of the Platonists (most likely the works of Plotinus or Porphyry rather than Plato himself). Keep in mind that Augustine's primary aim is to clarify his own metaphysical thoughts about God, the soul, and the origins of evil in the universe. Neo-Platonism was one of the most influential schools of thought in the ancient world, and it offered Augustine a metaphysical system that is not at all materialistic.

Although Augustine admires the metaphysical system of the Neo-Platonists, he frequently uses the word "proud" to describe them. While he believes that the Neo-Platonists may have the right ideas about the goal of human existence (union with a supremely good and perfect and spiritual God) they are completely wrong about the way to attain that goal. Augustine believes that they place far too much emphasis on the powers of reason and fail to appreciate the need for faith in Christ and submission to his Church. Augustine's attacks on Neo-Platonic thought are relatively consistent throughout his philosophical career, and all his criticisms center around the problem of pride or presumption, which he believes serves only to lead the Neo-Platonists away from God.

Having read selected books of the Neo-Platonists and having assimilated those insights that were more or less compatible with Christianity, Augustine describes how he was inspired to turn inward, away from all the noise and confusion of the sense world and enter into himself. The attempt ends in failure.[7.10-20]

Although Augustine acknowledges that the Neo-Platonists have a correct understanding of God as an infinite and incorporeal being, he also maintains that the Neo-Platonists fail to understand the right way to return to God. This is precisely the reason why Augustine views his own attempts to ascend to God in Milan as a complete failure. His own natural pride, magnified still further by his reading of the books of the Platonists, ensured that this vision could never be sustained.

Immediately following his encounter with the Neo-Platonists, Augustine describes how he was inspired to "snatch up" the epistles of Paul, which he claims had a powerful effect on him. It's clear that Augustine's aim is to contrast the difference between the philosophical approach to happiness that he had previously adopted and the more biblically and ecclesiastically oriented one that he would eventually come to adopt.[7.20]

But what is it that Augustine received from his reading of Paul that he could not have gotten simply from Neo-Platonism? Although he observes that everything he discovered in the books of the Platonists that was true he also finds in the writings of Paul, the truth that he discovers in Scripture is expressed "to the gift of [God's] grace."[7.21] For Augustine the philosopher it was necessary to submit to external authority in order to provide a remedy for his excessive pride. By submitting himself to legitimate authority Augustine is also acknowledging his own sinful state, his inability to follow God's law on his own and his need to be cared for by the collective body that is the Church.

Book 8 represents the immediate steps that led to Augustine's ultimate conversion in August of 386 AD. By this time, Augustine is aware that his is not a problem of intellectual certainty, but of moral stability. In order to attain this stability he needs to accept the way of the Savior—humble acceptance of his own moral infirmity and openness to the healing power of Christ—but he is unwilling to abandon the conviction of his own moral autonomy. "I was attracted to the way, The Savior himself," he says, "but I still hesitated to enter the narrowness of that path."[8.1]

In order to receive some guidance, Augustine goes to see Simplicianus, a bishop in Milan. Simplicianus tells Augustine the story of the conversion of Victorinus, who was a pagan noted for his translation of Neo-Platonic philosophical texts. The account inspires Augustine to following Victorinus' footsteps.[8.1-4]

Augustine may be "set on fire" to imitate Victorinus' example, but he finds himself being held back "by the iron chains of [his] own will."[8.5] Now that he is no longer a Manichean, he can't simply think that it was the "force of darkness" that was compelling him to sin against his own will. He now knows that he himself must ultimately be responsible for his own failings. But how can he account for the fact that he cannot simply will himself to stop sinning, even though he desires to do so?

To answer this question, Augustine devises his theory of the divided will. In general, an act of the will is quite simple. When it comes to moving a limb, for example, all one has to do is will the limb to move, and it does so automatically. Will and action here are one and the same. On the other hand, it is not quite so simple to think that we can overcome our illicit desires and inclinations, simply by willing them to disappear. I may desire to stop smoking, for example, but instead of being able to throw away my pack of cigarettes, I experience a conflict within my own will. I want to stop smoking, but I find myself incapable of doing so.

What is the reason for such a conflict? The answer, according to Augustine, is that I am not really desiring to do the good resolutely. Part of me wants to give up smoking, but another part doesn't really want to give up the pleasure of a nicotine rush. I am not completely sincere in my desire to stop smoking, so I lack a will that is unified enough to help me kick the habit.

The problem for Augustine is not that he does not want to follow God's law—his anguish over his moral failings clearly indicates that he does—but that he is not deliberate enough in his commitment to this law. In order for Augustine to overcome the division within his will, it is necessary for him to will resolutely and sincerely to follow God's law, and not in the half-hearted way that he had done so up until this point. Thus, he expresses a desire to be chaste and self-controlled, "but not yet."[8.7]

During this crisis, Augustine finds himself in a garden with Alypius, where he has resolved to settle once and for all the conflict within his soul. He describes himself as tortured over his inability to put aside lustful desires and finds himself growing progressively more ashamed of his own moral weakness.[8.8-9] In what is certainly the most artfully written section of the *Confessions*, Augustine creates an imaginary conflict within his own mind between the personifications of the objects of his lust, his mistresses of old, and that of "calm and serene" Continence. These objects of his lust (sex, power, wealth and fame) taunt him with the challenge of whether he can live without them. Implied in this taunt is the idea that if he cannot live without these lesser goods, then they, rather than God, have become the ultimate source of his delight.

At the same time, Augustine receives a vision of Continence, urging him towards an ordered love of worldly things. But how can he maintain an ordered love, when his will is still captivated by a disordered longing for worldly pleasure? The answer that Continence reveals to him is by not trying to rely on his own strength to accomplish this end, but rather by depending on God. Showing Augustine the images of men and women who have managed to give up worldly pursuits, Continence then reminds him that the strength they have to forsake the ways of the flesh is not their own doing.[8.11]

The choice that Augustine is faced with at this crucial juncture of the *Confessions*, then, is whether to continue along the path of presumption—the path of philosophy and of self-autonomy—and, in doing so, continue to fall prey to the force of habit; or whether to humbly implore the aid of the Liberator, forsaking the pride that has been the central driving force of his life until this point.

In the midst of this crisis—Augustine's confidence in the power of his own will at its lowest point in the *Confessions*—he tearfully throws himself under "a certain fig tree," and in utter desperation pleads for divine assistance. At that very moment he hears the voice of a child, which he interprets as a divine admonition. [8.12]

Upon receiving this admonition, Augustine shares his experience with Alypius, who coincidently is going through his own crisis. Upon opening the same text, Alypius receives a similar admonition, with the result that he too is strengthened in his resolve to follow God's law. Both decide immediately to put aside thoughts of marriage and a secular career and decide to enter the Church.

Related Readings

Augustine. "Evil as a Corruption of the Good"
Augustine. "Human Freedom and Punishment"
Plotinus. "The Ascent Towards the One
Acts of the Apostle. "The Conversion of St. Paul"

BOOK 6

The Beggar Analogy [6.6]

6. I hungered after honors, money, and marriage, but you were laughing at me the whole time. In chasing after those desires, I endured bitter difficulties, but you were ever so gracious in not allowing me to find anything sweet that wasn't you. Peer into my heart, Lord, for it was you who wanted me to remember this and to confess it. Having freed my soul from the sticky snare of death, let it now cling to you. How tortured it was! You probed to the very depths of the wound of my soul so that it might leave everything else behind and return to you who are above all things and without whom nothing else would exist; so that it might turn to you and be healed.

I remember how miserable I was then and how you made me aware of my misery on the very day when I was preparing to deliver a speech of praise to the emperor—one that was to include a multitude of lies that would be applauded by those who were well-aware of what I was doing. The stress of having to do the speech made my mind reel with the . . . destructive force of anxiety.

As I walked down one of the streets in Milan, I noticed a poor beggar. He was already drunk, it seemed, and he was laughing and enjoying himself. I groaned and pointed out to the friends I was with about how many difficulties resulted from our own insanities. In all our efforts . . . all we really wanted was to have the same kind of carefree enjoyment that the beggar had and which we might never attain. With just a handful of coins he had gathered by begging, he had already attained the kind of temporal happiness that I was struggling to reach through devious and muddled ways. Although his joy was not true joy, it was a great deal truer than the joy I was seeking in my ambitiousness. He was happy, while I was anxious; he was carefree while I was quaking with fears.

If anyone had asked me whether I would want to be happy or fearful, I would have answered "happy." If, on the other hand, someone had asked me whether I preferred to be a person like he was or the kind of person I was then, I would have chosen to be myself, with all the anxieties and fears that my lifestyle entailed. How absurd! Upon what basis would I have made such a choice? I might have said that my preference was based upon the fact that I was educated, but that wasn't a source of joy for me, but merely a way of impressing other people. I wasn't trying to teach them, but only to dazzle them, and this is why you battered my bones with the rod of your discipline.

I have no use for those who would say to my soul: "There's a difference in the source of a person's pleasure. The beggar found his in drink, while you were looking to find yours in glory." But what sort of glory is there, Lord, in a glory not found in you. Just as the beggar's glory wasn't real, so neither was mine, and it had an even worse effect on my mind. The beggar was able to sleep off his drunkenness that same night, while I slept and rose with mine day in and day out.

Certainly, the source of a person's happiness makes a difference. I know that. The joy of faithful hope is incomparably better than that such empty enjoyment. But even at that time, the beggar was far ahead of me: he was happier, and not only because he was soaked in merriment while I was flooded by anxiety: he had acquired his wine by spouting a few pleasant words to passers-by, while I was seeking swollen success by telling lies.

This is basically what I said to my close friends at the time, and I noticed that it was the same for them as it was for me. I felt awful, and my worry about my state made me feel twice as bad. If good fortune seemed to smile upon me, I didn't even try to grab hold of it, because, almost as soon as I could grasp it in my hands, it would fly away.

The Story of Alypius [6.7 - 6.10]

7. Those of us who were living together as friends used to grieve over these sorts of things, and I used to discuss them most often and most intimately with Alypius and Nebridius. Alypius came from the same town as me and his parents were leading citizens there. He was younger than me, and was a student of mine, first in our town and then later at Carthage. He was very fond of me be-

cause I seemed to him to be upstanding and educated, while I was attached to him because of his great virtue, which was evident even when he was very young.

But the whirlpool of Carthaginian vices and the lure of frivolous shows, sucked him in to the games put on at the circus. At the same time, he was unhappily involved with that, I was a professor of rhetoric and was teaching publicly. But he didn't attend my classes yet, because of a quarrel that had arisen between me and his father. I had heard about his harmful attachment to the games and was greatly distressed by it, because it seemed to me that he . . . was in danger of squandering his tremendous potential. But I had no means of restraining him by any kind of pressure, either through the benevolence of a friend or the authority of a teacher. I had supposed that he had the same opinion of me as his father, but that wasn't the case. So, he ignored his father's wishes and began to greet me when we met. He would also come to hear me lecture, staying for part of the lecture and then leaving.

I had by that point forgotten about my resolution to try to dissuade him from ruining his fine talent by such a reckless attachment to such empty pastimes. But you, Lord, who sits at the helm of everything you've created, did not forget him, who would one day be [ordained your priest]. His conversion should really be attributed to you, even though you brought it about through my unconscious efforts.

Here's how it happened.

One day when I was sitting as usual with my students in the classroom, Alypius walked in, greeted me, sat down, and gave his attention to what we were studying. While I was lecturing on a particular text, it occurred to me . . . that I could drive home my point more humorously by making fun of those who were enslaved by the games. You know, God, that at that time I had no thought about trying to cure Alypius of that disease. But he took my remarks personally and believed that I had said them exclusively with him in mind. Another person may have used this as an excuse for being angry with me, but this good young man became angry with himself and loved me all the more warmly for my remarks . . . After hearing my words, he pulled himself out of that pit in which he had been sinking . . . and with a great self-control he shook himself free of the filth of the games. He never attended the circus again after this . . .

10. . . . This was the kind of person Alypius was at the time, when he closely attached to me. And like me he struggled with uncertainty about the right way to live his life . . .

Efforts at Moral Conversion [6.11 - 6.16]

11. Looking back over my life, I was quite astonished at how much time had passed since my nineteenth year, when I had first been inflamed with the passion for wisdom and resolved that, when I found it, I would lay aside all the vain hopes, empty desires, and illusionary follies. But here I was already thirty and still stuck in the same muck of indecision, filled with greedy enjoyment for momentary things, which eluded me and wasted my soul. And all the time I kept saying, "Tomorrow I'll find it. It will appear plainly, and I'll grasp it" . . .

Even as I talked to myself in this way, the winds of uncertainty blew this way and that, pushing my heart in different directions. Time passed by but I still delayed in turning to the Lord. I postponed my life in you, but I could not postpone the fact that each day I was dying to myself. I longed for the happy life, but I feared finding it in its true place, fleeing from it even as I sought after it. I thought I would be much too miserable if I didn't have a woman's arms around me. I didn't think of the medicine of your mercy that could heal that infirmity, because I never tried it. I believed that sexual continence was something that had to be achieved by one's own strength, which I didn't believe I had. I was so foolish that I didn't know, as it is written in scripture, that no man can preserve his chastity, unless it is given to him by you. You would certainly have given it to me if I had pleaded to you with my inward groaning and with firm faith had cast my cares upon you.

12. It was Alypius who discouraged me from marrying. He kept saying that if I married there'd be no way that we could live together in untroubled leisure and devote ourselves to the pursuit of wisdom, as we had desired for so long. In sexual matters, he himself was completely chaste to a surprising extent. In his adolescence, he had engaged in sexual intercourse, but, far from being aroused by the experience, found it revolting and unpleasant.

Since then, he lived in perfect chastity.

I argued against him, citing the example of those, who though married pursued wisdom, served God, and maintained devoted and loving friendships. Of course, I could never match such men in nobleness of spirit. I was imprisoned of the sick disease of the flesh but feared to be free of it. And so I ignored his sound advice. ...Whenever the subject came up between us, I told him that I was completely incapable of living a celibate life. I used to defend myself when confronted by his astonishment at this, by saying that there was a great deal of difference between the hurried and secretive experience of his—which he could now barely remember and could easily dismiss—and the delights of my own long-term sexual relations with a woman. If the honorable name of marriage were added to this, I told him, he could have no reason to be surprised by my unwillingness to reject such a way of life....

13. I continued to be pressured to get married. I had already made a proposal and a girl was promised to me through my mother's efforts. She hoped that once I was married, I would be washed in the saving waters of baptism. To her great happiness, she saw me becoming more fit for this each day, observing that all her desires and your promises were being fulfilled in my faith . . . Pressure was kept up, but the girl for whom the offer was made was two years under the legal marriage age. I liked her, though, so I was willing to wait.

14. My friends and I would talk among ourselves, often expressing dissatisfaction with the turbulent troubles of human life. We had almost decided to withdraw ourselves from human society, living a life of peaceful contemplation. To accomplish this end, we decided that we would pool our resources and create a common household fund. In the spirit of sincere friendship, we decided that nothing would belong to any particular individual, but that that everything would count as one piece of property ... and everything would belong to everyone.

We thought that we could form a community of about ten people or so, some of whom were extremely rich—most notably Romanianus. He had come from our hometown to the court at Milan because of some troubles with his business dealings and had been a most intimate friend of mine since childhood. He was extremely enthusiastic about this project and his voice carried great weight, since he had more resources than the rest of us . . . But when the time came to discuss whether to admit to our community the wives that some of us already had and some of us looked forward to having, the whole plan fell apart . . .

15. Meanwhile, my sins were multiplying. The woman I was living with was torn from my side, because she was seen as an impediment to marriage. My heart which was deeply attached to her was torn, wounded, and left trailing blood. She returned to Africa, vowing to you that she would never be with another man and leaving me with the son I had fathered with her. But I, unhappily, was unable to follow in that woman's example. Having to wait two years until I could get the girl I was arranged to marry, I chafed at the delay. Not so much a lover of marriage as a slave to lust, I got myself another woman—not a wife, of course. Through this arrangement, the disease of my soul was fed and kept alive....

16. Praise and glory to you, O fountain of mercy. As I grew more and more miserable, you drew closer to me. Your right hand was by me, ready to pluck me out of the muck and wash me clean, though I didn't know it yet. Nor did anything call me back from the deep abyss of carnal pleasure, except the fear of death and the judgment to come, which never left my heart, despite all my changes of opinion . . .

What torture this was! How wretched was my soul in hoping to find something better than you. Turned this way and that, back and forth, from side to side . . . it could find no rest, for you alone are the only rest.

Just look! You're here, freeing us from our unhappy wanderings. You set us on your course, bringing hope and saying, "Run and I'll carry you. I'll lead you and I'll bring you to your journey's end."

BOOK 7

Speculations About the Nature of God [7.1 - 7.2]

1. By now, my evil and wicked youth was a thing of the past. I was becoming a man, but the older I became, the more foolish I had become. I was unable to entertain the idea of any kind of substance other than that which could be seen with my eyes. I was no

longer conceiving of you, God, in the shape of some human body. From the moment I started studying philosophy, I had rejected that notion, and I was glad to find the same kind of rejection in the faith of our spiritual mother, your Catholic Church. But no alternative way of thinking of you entered my mind. I, a mere man, and a flawed man at that, was trying to understand you, the only and true God.

With my whole heart I believed that you weren't subject to decay, injury or change. Although I didn't know why or how, I still saw quite clearly that what can decay is inferior to what can't decay, and what can't be injured is preferable to what can be injured, and what never changes is better than what changes. My heart cried out against all the phantoms crowding my mind, and I sought to drive away the swarms of unclean fantasies flying about there. No sooner than they had been scattered than they reemerged and were back again, invading and clouding over my vision. So, even though I no longer thought of you in the form of a human body, I was still forced to imagine something material out in space, whether infused into this world or diffused infinitely outside it. And this substance I saw as incorruptible, invisible, and unchangeable, which I saw as superior to the corruptible, visible, and changeable. I couldn't deny you some sort of dimensions, because anything lacking such dimensions seemed to be nothing at all, absolutely nothing, not even a void . . . And so I conceived of you, life of my life, as some kind of great substance spread out in every direction, infused throughout the whole world, and extending beyond it unbounded . . .

This was my belief, because I couldn't think about you in any other way. But it was false, because, according to this view a greater or lesser part of the world would contain a greater or lesser part of you. All things would be full of you, but in such a way that an elephant's body would contain a greater portion of you than a sparrow's, because it's larger and occupies more space. So, bit by bit you would be distributing yourself throughout the world, with large portions of you in large parts and small portions of you in small parts. Of course, that's not really how you exist, but you hadn't yet lightened my darkness.

2. As for the Manichaeans, those deceived deceivers and dumb

prattlers (dumb because they never had a word of yours to say), I had an excellent argument to counter them. The argument was put forward by Nebridius long before Carthage, and, when we heard it, we were all struck by it.

The Manichaeans postulated a force of darkness in opposition to you. But what could this force of darkness have done to you if you had refused to fight against it? If they replied that you would have been harmed, that meant that you were capable of experiencing injury and were destructible. If, on the other hand, they admitted that no harm could be done to you, then there would be no need to fight against this force . . . And so, if they maintain that in your real nature . . . you are incorruptible, then all these theories of theirs are shown to be untruths and to be scorned; but if they maintain that you are corruptible, then that very statement itself, as soon as it is uttered, becomes false and contemptible.

This argument of Nebridius was quite sufficient against the Manichaeans, whose beliefs I should have vomited from my overloaded stomach, for they had no possible escape from his dilemma without thinking and speaking of you with the most horrible blasphemes of mind and tongue.

Struggling with the Problem of Evil [7.3 - 7.5]

3. But a problem still remained for me. Although I would now say that you, our Lord and true God, . . . were immune to defilement and change, . . . I still couldn't grasp the cause of evil. Whatever it might be, though, I was determined that my inquiry wouldn't lead me to believe that the unchangeable God was changeable, since that would turn me into the very evil I was trying to investigate. . . .

I struggled to understand what I had heard—that our own free will was the cause of the evil we do and that your judgment is the cause of the evil we suffer. I couldn't grasp this clearly . . . But I was lifted towards your light by the fact that I was certain I had a will and that I had life. So, when I willed to do or not do something, I was completely confident that it was I who was doing the willing or not willing. And I began to see that the cause of my sin lay there.

But that with respect to that which I did against my will, it seemed to be something I suffered rather than did, and I judged it to be a punishment rather than a fault. Of course, I couldn't acknowledge that I was being punished unjustly, since I held you to be just.

Then I asked, "Who made me? Wasn't it my God, who is not only good but goodness itself? How was it possible then that I could will evil and resist good? Is it to provide a reason why it would be just to punish me? Who was it that set and sowed this bitter seedbed in me, seeing that I was made wholly by my sweet God? If the devil is responsible, where did the Devil come from? If he was by his own perverse will transformed from a good angel into a devil, what was the origin of the evil in him whereby he became a devil, seeing that he had been made an angel by that most good creator?

It was with thoughts like these that I was pushed down again and nearly suffocated. But I was not brought down so low as to dwell in that hell of error, where no one confesses to you and where it is believed that evil is something imposed upon you rather than something we commit.

4. In this manner, I attempted to find out even more, in the same way that I had already discovered that the incorruptible was better than the corruptible. On that basis I was ready to admit that, whatever you are, you are incorruptible . . . This admission . . . was where I needed to begin my inquiry to discover where evil is—that is, to discover the origin of that corruption which in no way can affect our God. For corruption cannot infect our God by will, necessity or chance, since he is God and what he wills is good and he himself is goodness. But to be corrupted is not good . . .

5. So I searched for the origins of evil, but I searched in the wrong way . . . I imagined your finite creation filled with your infinite being. And I said, "Here's God and here's what God has created, and he is good, supremely so, and better than all the things he created. And so, being good, he created all these things good, surrounding them and filling them . . . Where does evil come from, then, since a good God made all these good things? . . .

These were the kinds of thoughts that I was turning over in my unhappy heart, weighed down by the thought that death might overtake me before I had discovered the truth. Yet faith in Christ, our Lord and savior, professed in the Catholic Church, remained constant in my heart, even though this faith in many ways was still unformed and often swerved from the rule of right doctrine. Nevertheless, my mind didn't abandon it, but drank it in more and more deeply each day . . .

The Books of the Platonists [7.8 - 7.9]

8. You, Lord, abide forever and are not angry with us forever, because you have pity on our dust and ashes. And so, it was pleasing to you to reform my deformities. Inwardly, you stirred my soul and made me restless, until you could become clear to me. Through the healing power of your secret medicine, you settled my swelling, and day by day, the troubled eyesight of my soul... began to become cleared.

9. At first, you wanted to show me how you resist the proud but give grace to the humble. How great was your mercy in showing humanity the way of humility in your Word becoming flesh and dwelling among us. And so, by means of an enormously conceited man I knew, you brought to my attention certain books of the Platonists translated from Greek into Latin.

And I read in these works, not in the exact same words but to the same effect: "In the beginning was the Word and the Word was with God, and the Word was God. He was in the beginning with God. All things were made by him and without him nothing was made. What was made in him was life, and the life was the light of mankind. And the light shone in the darkness, and the darkness did not grasp it" . . . But I didn't find in these books of the Platonists that "he came into his own and the world did not receive him; but he gave to those who received him the power to become the sons of God—those that is who believed in his name."

I also read in these books that "the Word was not born of flesh or blood, nor the will of man, nor the will of the flesh, but of God." But I didn't read that "the Word was made flesh and dwelt among us."

I also observed in these books it was often stated in various different ways that "the Son was the form of the Father and [equal to the Father]." But I didn't read that "he emptied himself, taking on the form of a servant and was made in the likeness of man." Or that "he humbled himself even unto death . . . on the cross, and that God [raised] him from the dead . . . so that every tongue should confess that Jesus Christ is the glory of God the Father." ...

The Platonic Vision [7.10 - 7.20]

10. By these books I was admonished to return to myself. With you being my guide, I entered into my innermost self, and I was able to do that because you were my helper. I entered and saw with my soul's eye, such as it was, an unwavering light shining over and above that eye and above my mind. It was not ordinary light visible to those with a body; nor was it the same sort of light only brighter. It was a different thing entirely from any light of ours. This light transcended my mind, but not like oil floats on water or like the heavens are above the earth. It was superior because it made me, and I was inferior because I was made by it. Whoever knows the truth knows this light, and whoever knows this light knows eternity. Love knows it.

Oh, eternal truth, eternal love, beloved eternity! You are my God, and for you I sigh day and night. When I first came to know you, you lifted me up so that I could see that there was something to see in you, even if I couldn't yet see it. You beat the infirmity of my sight, shining your beams of radiance upon me, and I trembled with love and awe.

I found myself to be far away from you, in a land completely unlike yours . . . And I recognized that you discipline human beings to correct them for their sins, causing my soul to waste away like a spider's web . . . And I said, "truth can't be nothing because it is spread out neither in finite nor infinite space." But you cried out from afar, "In truth, I am who I am." I heard this in the way something is heard in the heart, and there was now no way I could doubt it. I would have found it easier to doubt that I was alive than that the truth existed . . .

11. And I reflected upon those things which are below you and saw that they had neither absolute being nor no being at all. They exist because they come from you, but they also are not because

they are not what you are. That which truly exists is that which exists unchangeably . . .

12. And it was evident to me that even things prone to corruption are good. They wouldn't be subject to corruption if they were either supremely good or not good at all. For, if they were supremely good, they would be entirely incorruptible; and, if there was no good in them at all, there would be nothing capable of being corrupted. Corruption is harmful, but it can only do harm if it diminishes what is good. It follows, then, that either corruption does no harm, which is impossible, or that all things that are corrupted suffer some privation of the good in them. This solution seems completely certain. If, however, they were deprived of *all* good, they would cease to exist. For if they still exist and were incapable of being corrupted, they would be better than before, because they would remain permanently incorruptible. What could be more absurd than to suggest that things could become better by losing all their goodness. So, if they're deprived of all good, they would be nothing at all.

Therefore, whatever exists must be good, and the evil whose source I was searching for cannot be a substance, because if it were, it would be good. Either it would be an incorruptible substance, and, therefore, one of the highest sorts of goods, or a corruptible substance, which could only be corrupted if it were good . . .

17. And I was astonished to discover that I had come to love you and not some phantom instead of you. But I couldn't rest steadfastly in the enjoyment of my God. I was caught up by your beauty, but swept away by my own weight, crashing back downwards towards inferior things. This weight was my carnal habit . . .

18. I tried to find the strength I needed to enjoy you, but I couldn't find it until I embraced that mediator between God and man—the man Jesus Christ, who is also above all things, blessed God forever more. He called out to me and said, "I am the way, the truth, and the life" . . . But I was not humble enough to accept the humble Jesus as my God, nor did I yet understand what his weakness had to teach. Your Word, eternal truth, which towers above all creation, raises up to itself only those who are submissive . . .

19. But I had a much different view at the time, conceiving my

Lord Christ simply as a man of excellent wisdom who none could equal . . . [I thought that] he deserved great authority as a teacher, but I hadn't yet begun to grasp the mystery contained in "The Word was made flesh" . . .

20. At this time, after having read the books of the Platonists, which taught me to seek a truth that was immaterial, I turned my attention towards your invisible reality which is understood through created things. I was pulled away again, but I did perceive how it was the darkness of my mind that hindered this understanding.

I was now certain that you were infinite, though not in the sense of being infinitely diffused through finite space, and that you existed in the fullest sense because you've always been the same . . .

Of these things I was certain, but I was still too weak to enjoy you. I prattled on as though I was a finished scholar, but unless I had sought the way to you through Christ our savior, I would have been completely finished. I wanted to come across to others like a wise scholar, but my punishment was within me. I didn't weep, but rather was inflated by my own knowledge. Where was the love that builds upon the foundation of humility, which is Jesus Christ? How were those books of the Platonists ever going to teach me that?

Yet I believed that you wanted me to come to these books before I turned to study your scriptures. You wanted me to remember the impression these books made upon me, so that afterwards when I was tamed by your books and my wounds healed by your gentle doctoring, I would be able to see clearly just how great a difference there was between presumption and confession—between those who saw the goal, but not the way to get there, and those who see the way to our blessed homeland and know how to live in it.

If I had come upon your scriptures first, with you growing sweet to me through familiarity with them, and then came upon these philosophical texts afterwards, it's very possible that they would have torn me from the strong roots of piety. Or, if I had held firm to the wholesome disposition that I had absorbed, I might have supposed that I could have gotten the same results from these philosophical books, had I studied them exclusively.

The Pauline Alternative [7.21]

21. So I greedily seized upon the writings of your spirit and especially upon those of the apostle Paul. In the past, it sometimes seemed to me that he contradicted himself or that his teachings conflicted with the testimonies of the law and the prophets, but as I read, these difficulties vanished away. I now saw just once face in that verbal eloquence and was delighted to the point of trembling. I began reading and discovered that whatever truth I had found in those philosophical works was also found here, but it was expressed in terms of the gift of your grace. This is to keep anyone who sees it from bragging, as though he hasn't been given, not just what he sees, but the very ability to see as well. For "who has anything that he has not received?" . . .

[And I read that] even though a person may be delighted with God's law, "what will he do with that other law in his body, which is at war with the law of his mind, and which keeps him captive to sin? . . . What shall this wretched man do? Who shall deliver him from this body of death, unless it is through the grace of Jesus Christ our Lord?" . . .

None of this is to be found in those books of the Platonists. There's nothing in those pages about the face of pity, the tears of confession, your sacrifice, the troubled spirit, the broken and contrite heart, the salvation of your people, the bridal city, the earnestness of the Holy Spirit, the cup of redemption.

No one in those books sings, "Shall not my soul wait upon God. For he is my God, my savior, and my protector. I shall waver no longer." No one there hears him call out, "Come to me all you who labor." They are too proud to hear from him, because he is gentle and humble of heart. You've hidden these things from the wise and clever but have revealed them to little children.

It's one thing to see from a forested mountaintop the land of peace, but not to find the way there, struggling in vain through unpassable ways, ambushed and assaulted on all sides by fugitive deserters led by the lion and the dragon. It's quite another thing to hold to the way that leads there, on a road defended by the heavenly general. No deserters from the heavenly army lie waiting to attack, for they avoid that way like a torture.

In marvelous ways these things affixed themselves to my innermost being as I read the least of your apostles. I meditated upon your works and I trembled.

BOOK 8

Prayer [8.1]

1. In a spirit of gratitude, O my God, let me remember and confess to you the mercies you have granted me. Let my bones be penetrated with your love, and let them cry out to you, "Who is like you, O Lord?" You have completely broken my bonds; let me offer you a sacrifice of praise. I will tell how you have severed these shackles, so that all who worship you, when they hear my tale, will say, "Blessed be the Lord, in heaven and in earth, for great and wonderful is his name."

Your words had now firmly fixed themselves in my heart, and I was besieged on all sides by you. I was quite certain now of your eternal life, though I saw it obscurely, as through a looking glass. But I no longer doubted that there was an incorruptible substance from which all other substances were derived. And I no longer desired to be more certain of you, but only to stand more firmly in you. As for my temporal life, everything was in a state of flux, and my heart needed to be purged of its old ways. I was attracted to the way, the Savior himself, but I still hesitated to enter the narrowness of that path . . .

The Example of Victorinus [8.1 - 8.4]

You put it into my mind, and it seemed a good idea to me, that I should go to visit Simplicianus. I thought of him as your good servant—a man from whom your grace radiated. I had also heard that from his youth he had lived a life completely devoted to you. Since he was an old man by now and had spent so many years following your way with great zeal, he appeared to be a man of much experience and learning. And that's exactly what he was. I wanted to consult with him about my troubles, to see if he could offer some direction for a man like me to walk in your path.

The church I saw was full of people going in their various ways. I was unhappy with the life I was leading in the world, which was a great burden to me. I wasn't burning any longer with the desire for fame and money. By this time those enticements no longer held any delight when compared with the sweet wholesomeness of your church to which I was greatly attached.

But I was still enthralled by the love of a woman. The apostle didn't forbid me to marry, although he advised me to do better and strongly wished that all men were unattached as he was. But I, being weak, chose a softer place. Because of this, I was disturbed in other areas of my life, wasting away with constant cares. I was forced to content with numerous other anxieties, because they went along with the married life. In my commitment to that I was restricted in my other options . . .

2. So I went to see Simplicianus, who once acted as a kind of father to Bishop Ambrose in receiving your grace, and Ambrose truly loved him like a father. I described the winding course of my erroneous ways to him. I mentioned to him that I had read some of the books of the Platonists, translated into Latin by Victorinus, who was at one time a professor of rhetoric in Rome, who had, I heard, died a Christian. He congratulated me that I had not stumbled upon the writings of other philosophers, whose works were full of fallacies and deceits, . . . whereas in the Platonic works God and his Word are everywhere implied. Then to exhort me to Christ's humility, hidden from the wise and revealed to the little ones, he reminisced about Victorinus himself, whom he had known intimately while he was in Rome. I won't keep silent about the story he told me, for this story gives me the opportunity to testify in great praise of your grace . . .

The story, as Simplicianus told it to me, was that Victorinus was in the habit of studying scripture and all other Christian writings with the most exacting attention. After examining them, he said to Simplicianus (not in public but in private, intimate conversation), "You know, I'm already a Christian." Simplicianus replied, "I won't believe that or consider you a Christian until I see you in the Church of Christ." Victorinus smiled and replied, "Is it the wall that makes Christians?"

It would happen often that Victorinus would claim to be a Christian. Simplicianus would respond in the same way, and Victorinus would repeat his joke about the walls. In fact, he was afraid of offending his influential [pagan] friends . . . But later he gained courage from his deep reading, and came to fear that he might be disowned by Christ in the company of his holy angels if he refused to confess before men and women. ... Suddenly and unexpectedly, he said to Simplicianus, "Let's go to the Church. I want to become a Christian." Simplicianus, who could not contain his joy, went along with him . . . Not long afterwards, he gave in his name, requesting rebirth in baptism—to the amazement of Rome and the joy of the Church . . .

When the time came for him to make his profession of faith, custom decreed that these words were to be recited on an elevated platform before the assembly of your believers . . . Simplicianus told me that Victorinus had been offered by priests the option of making his profession in private, as was the custom for some shy people who were liable to become frightened, but that he chose rather to proclaim his salvation in the sight of the holy congregation . . .

When he climbed up the platform to make his profession, everyone who knew him proclaimed his name to one another in a clamor of congratulations. And who there, didn't know him? From the lips of the whole body came a soft whisper: "It's Victorinus; it's Victorinus." Quickly they grew noisy with the excitement of seeing him, but soon settled down so they could hear him. And with great confidence, he proclaimed his true faith . . .

4. Come Lord, arouse us and call us back! Set us on fire and pull us towards you! Let your sweet fragrance grow upon us. Let us love you, let us run to you . . .

The Two Wills [8.5, 8.7]

5. When your man Simplicianus told me this story about Victorinus, I was set on fire to emulate him—which is precisely the reason why he told me this story. He also told me how in the days of the Emperor Julian, when there was a law passed forbidding Christians from teaching literature and rhetoric, Victorinus welcomed the law and preferred to abandon the chattering classroom than to abandon your Word, which make even the tongues of infants eloquent. In this, he seemed to me to be more lucky than courageous, because he found the opportunity to dedicate all his time to you. I longed for such freedom myself, but I was bound

not by irons imposed upon me by anyone else, but by the iron chains of my own will.

The enemy held my will, and made a chain out of it, and bound me with it. For from a perverse will came lust, and lust given into became habit, and habit not resisted became necessity. These links, as it were, joined together—for this reason I called it a chain—and held me fast in harsh slavery. But that new will, which had begun to develop in me, freely to serve you and to enjoy you, O God, was not yet able to overcome the old will, which had become strengthened by long custom. And so, my two wills—one new and the other old, one carnal and the other spiritual—struggled within me; and they laid waste to my soul by their discord.

Thus, I understood by my own experience what I had read—that the flesh lusts against the spirit and the spirit against the flesh. I certainly was on both sides, but more when I was on that side which I approved in myself than on that side which I disapproved. For the latter was not really "me," because, for the most part, I suffered things against my will rather than doing them willingly. And yet it was my own fault that custom became more powerful against me, since I had come willingly where I now wished not to be. And who has any right to complain when just punishment overtakes the sinner?

Nor had I any longer my former excuse that the reason I continued to hesitate to turn my back to the world and serve you was because I could not see the truth clearly. For now I could see it with perfect clarity. But I was still bound to the earth and refused to be your soldier. I was as much afraid of being freed of my encumbrances as I was of being encumbered by them.

And so I was held down by the pleasant burdens of this world, like one who is asleep, and the thoughts in which I attempted to meditate on you were like the efforts of one who tries to wake up but who sinks back again into sleep. No one, of course, wants to sleep forever, and sensible people all agree that it is better to be awake; yet a man, feeling the sleepiness of his limbs, generally puts off waking up and, even after it is time to arise, often defers to shake off sleep, though he knows he should not be doing so. In the same way, I was quite sure that it was much better to give myself up to your charity than to give myself over to my own desires;

but though the former course satisfied me and was beginning to gain mastery over me, the latter pleased me and ensnared me. I didn't have any answer to give to you as you called out to me, "Awake, you who sleep, and arise from the dead, and Christ will give you light." And when you showed me in every possible way that what you said was true, I had no answer, except the dull and drowsy words, "A minute. Just a minute. Let me have just a little while longer." But these minutes never ended, and my little while went on for a very long while.

I tried unsuccessfully to delight in your law according to the inner man, while another law in my members rebelled against the law of my mind and led me captive under the law of sin which was in my members. For the law of sin is the strong force of habit, whereby the mind is drawn and held, even against its will—but deservedly, for the mind fell into the habit willingly. Who then shall deliver me, wretched man that I am, from the body of this death, but only your grace, through Jesus Christ our Lord? . . .

7. By now, I began to hate myself. . . . Many years—perhaps twelve—had already passed by since my nineteenth year, I was aroused to pursue wisdom by the reading of Cicero's *Hortensius*. And here I was, still postponing the abandonment of this world's happiness to devote myself to the search. Yet the search alone for wisdom, let alone finding it, would have been preferable to acquiring all the treasures and kingdoms of this world, or those bodily pleasures that were mine for the taking. I was a miserable young man, right from the start, and, as I prayed for the gift of your chastity, I would say, "Give me chastity and self-control, but not yet." I was afraid that you would hear me too soon and too quickly cure me of the disease of my lust, which I still preferred to satisfy rather than to extinguish.

I convinced myself that the reason for my delay in rejecting those worldly ambitions and following you alone was because I couldn't see any clear light by which to direct my course. But now the day had arrived in which I was stripped naked to myself and my conscience was to mock me: "Where is that tongue of yours now? You said that you were unwilling to cast off your illusions because the truth was uncertain. But now you have certainty and your burdens still oppress you. At the same time others who have not worn themselves out searching, people who have not spent a decade or more thinking about these things, have their shoulders unshackled and are given wings to fly."

. . . What was there left to say in this inner debate of mine? Was there any whip of shame that I didn't use to make my soul come along, as I struggled to follow after you? Yet it held back, resisted, and refused to make the effort. All of its arguments had been used up and repudiated, but there remained that unsettling fear—the fear of resisting that habit by which it was wasting itself to death.

The Struggle in the Garden [8.8 – 8.9]

8. In the midst, then, of this great quarrel of my inner dwelling, . . . disturbed both in mind and appearance, I rushed to Alypius and cried: "What's wrong with us? What is this that you have just heard? The unlearned are rising up and taking heaven, while we, with all our learning, are wallowing in the world of flesh and blood! Are we ashamed to follow because they have gone ahead of us? And aren't we ashamed of not having the courage to follow at all?" I spoke words like these, and the disturbance of my mind tore me away from him, while he gazed on in silent bewilderment. For I spoke in strange tones, and my forehead, cheeks, eyes, color, and tone of voice all expressed my emotions more fully than the words I had uttered.

There was a small garden attached to the house where we were staying. We were free to make use of it as well as the house, since the owner of the house, our host, was not living there. The turmoil in my heart had driven me to this garden, and no one would interfere with the debate I had started within myself until it could be resolved—the outcome of which you knew, though I did not. I only knew that I was going mad so that I might be whole, and dying that I might have life, knowing what an evil thing I was, but not knowing what a good thing I was soon to become.

I went into the garden, and Alypius followed behind me. My privacy was not lessened by his presence, and, in any case, how could he have abandoned me in the state that I was in? We sat down as far from the house as possible. I was troubled in spirit for not entering into your will and covenant, my God, which all my bones cried out to me to enter and praised it to the heavens. And the way to go there is not by ships, or chariots, or feet; nor did it even demand going so far as the short distance I had come from the house to the place where we were sitting. For to go there, all I had had to do was to will to go, but to will it resolutely and sincerely; not to toss and turn, this way and that of a will half-maimed by the struggle, with one part falling as another rose.

While still consumed by the fever of my irresoluteness, I made many bodily movements—the kind that people often want to perform, but cannot, either because they lack limbs, or because they are bound, or weakened by sickness, or in some other way prevented from acting. If I tore out my hair, beat my forehead, locked my fingers together around my knee, I did so because I willed it. But I might have willed to do so and not have done it, if the power of motion in my limbs had not obeyed. So, I did many things where "willing" was not the same as "being able." And yet I was not able to do the thing that I longed to do so much more, and which very shortly, when I willed it, would be able to do, because when I willed, I should will thoroughly. For in this particular instance the ability was one with the will, and to will was to do. And yet it was not done. It was much easier for my body to obey the weakest willing of my soul to move my limbs than it was for the soul to carry out its own major act of willing, which could be accomplished in the will alone.

9. What is the cause of this absurd situation? Let your mercy illuminate my inquiry, so that an answer can be found in the mysterious punishment of humanity and the darkest pains of the children of Adam. What is the cause, then, of this absurd situation? The mind commands the body, and the body obeys immediately; the mind commands itself and is resisted. The mind commands the hand to move, and so complete is the compliance that the command is hardly to be distinguished from its execution. Yet the mind is mind and the hand is body. The mind commands the mind—its own self—to will, and yet it does not. Again, what is the cause of this absurd situation? The mind, I say, commands itself to will something, and it would not command, unless it willed, and yet what it commands is not done. But it does not will the thing entirely, and therefore it does not command entirely. Insofar as it commands the thing, it does will it, but insofar as the thing is not done, it does not will it. For the will commands that there be a will—not a different will, but itself. But it does not

command entirely, and therefore the command is not obeyed. For if the will was entire, it would not command itself to act, since the will would already be there.

This partial willing and partial non-willing is not quite so absurd, but is rather a sickness of the soul, which was so weighed down by habit that it cannot be raised up by the truth. There are two wills, then, and neither is entire, because one has what the other lacks.

Rejection of the Manichaean Solution [8.10]

10. There are those who, having perceived two deliberating wills, conclude that there are two natures within us—one good and one evil. Let them perish from your presence, O God, as do all those idle talkers who lead our minds astray. They themselves are truly evil when they assert such things, and yet these same people could become good if they would just assent to the truth, so that your Apostle may say to them, "You were in darkness once, but now light in the Lord." Unfortunately, they want to be light, not in the Lord, but in themselves, and, imagining the nature of the soul to be that what God is, are made more gross darkness still through their dreadful arrogance; for they have moved further away from you, the true light that enlightens everyone who comes into the world. I say to these men, be wary of what you say and blush for shame; but draw near to him and be enlightened, and you shall no longer be ashamed.

When I was deliberating about whether to serve the Lord my God now, as I had long intended, I was the one who wanted to do it and I was also the one who wanted not to do it. I was the only one involved. But I neither willed this course entirely nor rejected it entirely. I was at war with myself and was torn apart by myself. This tearing apart took place against my will, but what it indicated was not the presence of an alien mind, but a punishment that I was suffering in my own mind. Therefore, it was not I who caused it, but the sin that dwelled within me—the penalty for a sin more freely committed, for I was a son of Adam.

For, if there are as many conflicting natures as there are conflicting wills, there would not be two such natures only, but many. Suppose a man is wondering whether he should go to the Manichaean assembly or to the theater. These Manichaeans will say, "You see, here are two natures, one good, pulling him in one direction, the other evil, pulling him in another. For what else could this indecision be except a conflict between wills?" But I say that both are equally bad—that which pulls towards them and that which pulls towards the theater. But they believe that a will which pulls towards them must be good.

But suppose one of us should deliberate, and through a conflict of his two wills, should be in confusion as to whether he should go to the theater or to our Church. Wouldn't these same Manichaeans be perplexed as to what to say on this point? For they must either confess that the will which leads to our Church is good as well as theirs (something they would not be willing to do); . . . or they must assume that in the same man there are two evil natures and two evil souls, and that it is not true, as they say, that there is one good and another bad; or they must be converted to the truth, and no longer deny that when a person is deliberating there is a soul fluctuating between two conflicting wills.

Let them stop saying, therefore, when they perceive two conflicting wills in the same man, that the conflict is between two opposing souls, of two opposing substances, from two opposing principles, one good and the other bad. For you, O God of truth, have disproved, checked, and overthrown them. Such is the case when both wills being bad, one debates whether he should kill a man by poison or by the sword; whether he should seize this or that part of a man's property, when he cannot have both; whether he should squander his money for pleasure or hoard his money like a miser; whether he should go to the circus or the theater, if both are opened on the same day (a third option being to rob another's house if he has the opportunity and a fourth being to commit adultery)—assuming he has the means to do all these things at the time, and all are equally desired, although impossible to enact at the same time. The mind is then torn apart by four or even more . . . conflicting wills. But the Manichaeans do not hold that there are a similar number of conflicting substances.

The same holds true in wills which are good. Let me ask: Is it a good thing to take pleasure in reading the apostle? Or a good thing to take pleasure in a sober psalm? Or a good thing to discuss the Gospel? For each of these, they will answer, "It is good." But what if all of these give equal pleasure at the same time? Doesn't this mean that different wills distract the mind, while he deliberates which to select? Yet they are all good, but they compete among themselves until one is chosen . . . It is likewise the case when eternity delights us from above and the pleasure of temporal goods holds us down from below: our one soul is not ready to embrace either with its entire will. And so the soul is torn apart with great distress, with truth pulling in one direction and habit pulling in the other.

Inner Debate [8.11]

11. This was what my sickness and torment was like. And I accused myself far more severely than I usually did, tossing and turning in my chain, as I strove to break free from it completely. I was held by it only slightly, but I was still held. And you, O Lord, pressed upon me in my innermost being by a severe mercy, redoubling the lashes of fear and shame, so that I would not give way once more, and that small piece of chain that still bound me would not get stronger and bind me even more. I said to myself, "Let it be done now, let it be done now." And as I spoke these words, I was all but moving in that direction. I nearly did it, but yet did not do it. But I didn't slip back into my own ways but took a breath and kept my stand. And I tried again . . . and all but touched and grasped it; and yet still I did not come to it, or touch it, or grasp it; for I hesitated to die to death and to live to life . . . At that very moment in which I was to become something other than I was, the nearer it approached me, the greater was my horror, but it did not strike me back, nor turn me away, but held me in suspense.

The very toys of toys and vanities of vanities, my ancient mistresses, were still holding me back, as they plucked the garment of my flesh and whispered softly, "Do you think you can be done with us? From this moment shall we no longer be with you forever? And from his moment shall this-and-that no longer be lawful for you forever?" And what did they suggest to me by "this" and "that"? What did they suggest, O my God? Let your mercy turn it away from the soul of your servant. What foul deed were they suggesting? What shameful acts? But now their voices were half as loud, and they did not openly show themselves to contradict me, but muttered, as it were, behind my back, and slyly grasping at me as I walked away to make me look back at them. And yet they did delay me as I hesitated to tear free and shake them off and move in the direction in which I was being called. They had an aggressive habit of taunting me by saying, "Do you really think that you can live without them?"

But now it spoke very faintly. For on that side where I had turned my face and where I hesitated to go, there appeared to me the chaste, dignified figure of Continence. She was serene and calm, honestly beckoning me to come and doubt no longer. As she stretched forth to receive and embrace me, her holy hands filled with multitudes of good examples of all ages, there were some young men and women here and grave widows and aged virgins. And in them all was Continence herself, not barren, but a fruitful mother of children, her joys given by you, her husband, O Lord. She smiled on me with encouraging prodding, as though to say, "Can't you do what these youths and maidens have done? Or do you think that they did it all by themselves and without the help of the Lord their God? The Lord their God gave me to them. Why do you insist upon standing by yourself, and so not really stand firm at all? Cast yourself upon him and fear not. He will not draw away and let you fall. Lean fearlessly upon him and he will receive you and heal you." And I was blushing with shame, for I could still hear the whisperings of those vanities of mine and hung back in suspense. And yet again she seemed to say, "Close your ears to those unclean parts of you that belong to the earth, so that they might be mortified. They might tell you of delights, but nothing like the delights that are told by the law of the Lord your God."

This debate within my heart was a struggle between myself and myself. But Alypius, sitting by my side, silently waited to see how this extreme agitation within me would end.

Augustine's Conversion [8.12]

12. But this deep reflection, from the secret depths of my soul, drew together and heaped up all my misery . . . , and there arose a great storm within me, bringing with it a mighty shower of tears. So that I might be free to give vent to these feelings without

self-consciousness, I left Alypius, since solitude was more appropriate for the act of weeping. I went far enough away that even his presence would not be a burden to me. This was how I was feeling, and he understood it; for I suppose that I had said something, and the tones of my voice must have appeared choked with tears. And so, I arose to leave, and he remained where we were sitting, filled with extreme astonishment. I threw myself down—I don't really know how—under a certain fig tree and gave full reign to my tears. They poured out from my eyes like a flood, an acceptable sacrifice to you. And, I said to you, not in these exact words, but in this sense, "And you, O Lord, how long? How long, Lord? Will you be angry forever? O do not remember our former sins." For I felt it was these that were holding me back. I uttered these cries of despair to you: "How long, how long this "tomorrow and tomorrow? Why not now? Why can't my depravity be put to an end at this every hour?"

I was saying words of this sort and crying in the bitter contrition of my heart, when suddenly a voice reached my ears from a nearby house. It was the voice of a boy or girl—I don't know which—and it kept repeating, "Take it and read. Take it and read." Immediately, my mood changed. I began to reflect upon whether words like these were ever used in the kinds of games that children play but couldn't remember ever before hearing words of that kind. I gained control over the flood of my tears and arose, interpreting it to be nothing other than a command from God to open the book and read the first chapter I came upon. For I had once heard that Anthony, coming in during the reading of the Gospels, believed the words to be directed to him, when he heard, "Go and sell all you have, and give the money to the poor, and you will have treasure in heaven, and come follow me." By such a divine message was he converted to you.

Eagerly, I then returned to the place where Alypius was sitting, since it was in that spot that I had left the book of the Apostle when I had gotten up. Snatching it up and opening it, in silence I read that section upon which my eyes first fell: "Not in rioting and drunkenness, not in debauchery and wantonness, not in strife and envying; but put on the Lord Jesus Christ, and make not provision for the flesh, in concupiscence." I didn't need to read any further, for immediately at the end of this sentence, the light of certainty flooded my heart, and the darkness of doubt vanished away.

I closed the book, and either using my fingers or some other means to mark the page, and with complete calmness told Alypius what had happened. And he told me in his turn what had been going on with him, which I didn't know anything about. He asked to see what I had read, and I showed him. And he looked beyond even what I had read. I didn't know the words that followed, which were, "He that is weak in faith, receive"—which he applied to himself and interpreted for me. He became strengthened by the admonition; and he joined me with the kind of strong resolution and commitment that was totally in keeping with his character (for in this respect he was quite superior to me).

We then went inside to my mother and told her what happened, and she rejoiced. We described to her what took place and she leapt with joyful triumph, and blessed you, who have the power to do much more than we ask for or understand. For she understood that you had given her much more in my regard than she had even asked for in her pitiful and sorrowful pleadings. For you had converted me to yourself, so that I no longer sought a wife or any worldly ambitions. I was now standing in that rule of faith that many years earlier you had shown to her in a vision of me. And, in doing so, you converted her sorrow into joy—a joy far more plentiful than she had desired, and much more precious and purer than she could have hoped for by having grandchildren from my flesh.

Beatitude and Beyond

Confessions 9.1 - 10.42

⌇⍀⊺⍀⌇

*C*onfessions 9 begins with yet another prayer extolling God's goodness and mercy and acknowledging the sinfulness of human beings. Through God's grace Augustine is set free from the enslavement to temporal goods.[9.1] He quietly withdraws from his profession as teacher of rhetoric, using health concerns as his excuse.[9.2]

A wealthy friend of his, Verecundus, offers Augustine the peace and quiet of his country estate at Cassiciacum in Northern Italy, where Augustine in September of 386 retreats with his mother, son and a few close friends. It's here that Augustine begins his career as a Christian philosopher, writing such important works as *The Happy Life* and *The Soliloquies*.[9.3 - 9.4]

Augustine returns to Milan in March of 387, where he, Alypius, and his son, Adeodatus, are all baptized. His happiness is slightly marred, however, by the death of his son a short time later.[9.6] The group decide to return to Africa to dedicate their lives to the service of God. On the way back to Thagaste, they stop at Ostia—a major port in Southern Italy—to await the boat to Africa.

While Augustine and Monica wait for the boat that would take them back to Ostia, Augustine describes how he and his mother were looking out upon a garden in the house where they were staying in Ostia. While they are reflecting on the joys of the next life, the two have a joint mystical experience.[9.10]

There's been much debate in scholarly writings on the *Confessions* about the differences between Augustine's unsuccessful attempt at mystical union after reading the books of the Platonists in Book 7 and the seemingly more successful attempt at Ostia in

Book 9. It shouldn't be at all surprising that Augustine views the end of the two experiences as being identical: we have already seen that for him philosophy and true religion can both lead the seeker of wisdom to one and the same promised land. The difference between the two, as we have also seen, lies, not so much in the *goal* that is sought, but in the *way* that it is sought. The reason why Augustine must continue his narrative is precisely because he wishes to distinguish between that type of vision that is the end-product of presumption (the vision at Milan) and that which is the end-product of confession (the vision at Ostia). The unique aspect of the vision, therefore, lies exclusively in the fact that it is the by-product of grace and is found only in a life of complete submission to the Church.

Despite the brevity and transient nature of the experience at Ostia, the moral results of this vision differ completely from that of the vision in Milan. As in the former vision, Augustine's soul ascends upward towards "that region of never-failing plenty," where he briefly intuits the bliss of heavenly existence, though barely touching it with the "whole strength of [his] hearts' impulse." The entire experience is described as "a moment of comprehension" and ends as suddenly as it began with Augustine's returning to his normal state. This time, however, the experience does not end in ever greater misery and despair, but rather in a profound sense of peace and hope. As opposed to the first vision, in which he is pulled away from God by the weight of his own carnal habit, the vision at Ostia reinforces his belief that the goods of the world, over which he had previously lusted, are nothing compared to the joy of resting in God for all eternity.

Shortly after their experience at Ostia, Monica falls into a fever and dies at the age of 56. Of course, Augustine is saddened by the death of his mother, but, unlike with the death of his nameless friend from Book 4, he is not inconsolable. His faith has given him a strength and a larger perspective that he did not have in 375, confident that his mother is resting securely in God and that he will join her eventually in the next life. [9.11-13]

If the *Confessions* ended at this point, it would be typical of the conversion accounts that preceded Augustine. In such accounts, the wayward Christian—mind illuminated by God, will purified by God, and given a taste by God of his essence in the beatific vision—commits himself totally to a life devoted to service to God and his church. There should be complete peace at this point in the narrative and absolute freedom from the sinful lures of the world. But Augustine is most certainly not the typical Christian thinker.

In Book 10 of the *Confessions*, he leaps from his memories of the past to the realities of the present.

At the end of Book 9, it is 386 AD and Augustine has left Italy to return home to North Africa, having been only recently baptized. When he begins to write the *Confessions*, it is a decade later and he is now Bishop of Hippo, a staunch defender of the faith against heresy, and already starting to become recognized as a profound Christian thinker.

But Augustine also believes that the soul won't find complete rest until it rests permanently in God. This world in Augustine's view will always be "an unending trial," a place where even God's chosen will be forced to endure incessant temptations. The difference is that now that Augustine is the recipient of God's grace, he can resist the temptation around him. And that, in the end, is the best that the Christian can hope for in this life.

Related Readings

Augustine. "The Grace of God"
Augustine. "The Effects of Grace."
Augustine. "Seeing God"
Augustine. "Eternal Life with God."

BOOK 9

Prayer [9.1]

1. O Lord, I am your servant; I am your servant and the son of your handmaid. You have broken my bonds. I will offer to you the sacrifice of thanksgiving. Let my heart and my tongue praise you, and let all my bones say, "Lord, who is there like you?" Let them say this, and answer me and say unto my soul, "I am your salvation."

Who am I and what am I? Is there any evil I haven't committed in my deeds, or, if not in my deeds, in my words, or, if not in my words, my will? But you, O Lord, are good and merciful, and your right hand reached into the depth of my death and emptied out the abyss of corruption from the bottom of my heart. And this was the result: now I stopped willing what I willed and began willing what you willed.

But where was my free will during all those years? And from what deep and secret place was it called forth in a single moment, so that I could bow my neck to your easy yoke and my shoulders to your easy burden, Oh Christ Jesus, my Strength and my Redeemer? How sweet did it suddenly become to me to be without the sweetness of those empty pleasures! How glad I was now to put away what I formerly feared to lose. For you cast these trifles away from me, Oh true and highest Sweetness. You cast them away, and in their place you entered yourself . . . Now my soul was free from the gnawing cares of ambition, wallowing in the filth, and scratching the itch of lust. And I prattled like a child to you, O Lord my God, my light, my riches, and my salvation.

Retiring from the World [9.2 – 9.6]

2. And so I decided that it would be pleasing in your sight to . . . withdraw quietly from my position [as a teacher of rhetoric], so that my students (who were not concerned about your law or your peace, but with ridiculous lies and court battles) might no longer buy from my mouth weapons for their own madness. Fortunately, there were only a few days left before the [holiday season], and I chose to endure those days, so that I might resign in due course

with proper formality. Then my freedom could be purchased by you and my skills no longer put up for sale. My plan was known, but it was not publicly known, except to a few friends, for we had agreed that it should not be made public . . .

You had pierced our hearts with your love, and we carried your words, as it were, thrust through our vitals. The examples of your servants whom you had changed from black to shining white, and from death to life, crowded into the bosom of our thoughts and burned and consumed our sluggish temper, so that we might not topple back into the abyss. And they fired us up, so that every breath of the deceitful tongue of our detractors might fan the flame and not blow it out . . .

During that summer my lungs had begun to weaken from too much scholarly labor, so that breathing became difficult. The pains in my chest showed that the lungs were affected, and this made it impossible for me to speak too loudly or for too long. At first, this worried me, because it appeared that this condition would either force me to give up my teaching career . . . or at least taking time off for rest. But now that I had become firmly committed to the idea of [serving you], I began to rejoice a having a genuine excuse to soften the displeasure of those parents whose concerns for their sons educations would have never permitted me to leave my position.

Full of joy, then, I endured this interval until my time ran out—perhaps some twenty days or so—yet even this took some effort on my part, because I no longer had interest in the money which had formerly sustained the heavy burden of my work. Had not patience taken its place, I would have been crushed by my labors. . . .

4. Finally the day came on which I was actually to be relieved from the professorship of rhetoric, from which I was already freed in spirit. Now it became a reality. And you rescued my tongue as you had already rescued my heart. I blessed you for it with great joy and left with my friends to the country house . . .

When would there be enough time to record all the great blessings which you did bestow on us in that time, especially now that I am hurrying on to even greater mercies? My memories recall that period and it pleases me to confess to you, Lord, how you goaded and tamed me, . . . and how you laid low my proud intellect . . .

5. When the vacation period was over, I gave notice to the cit-

izens of Milan, so that they could find another word merchant for
their students. The reasons I gave were that I had decided to serve
you and that I had insufficient strength for the position, because
of difficulty breathing and the pain in my chest. I also wrote to
your bishop Ambrose of my past errors and my present desires
and asked his advice as to which books of yours I should read to
prepare myself for grace and to be better able to receive it. He
recommended the prophet Isaiah, because he foretold the Gospels
and the calling of the Gentiles more clearly than all the other writers. But because I could not understand the first part of the text
and imagined the rest to be like it, I laid it aside with the intention
of taking it up again later, when better trained in our Lord's words.

6. When the time arrived for me to give in my name for baptism, we left the country and returned to Milan. Alypius also decided to be born again in you at the same time. He was already
clothed with the humility that befits your sacraments and had already tamed his body to such an extent that he would walk bare-
foot over the frozen Italian soil.

We also took with us the boy Adeodatus, the son after the flesh,
sinfully begotten by me. You turned him into a fine boy. He was
barely fifteen years old, but his intelligence already surpassed that
of many serious and well-educated men. I acknowledge these to
be your gifts, O Lord my God, creator of all things, who has power to reform our deformities, for there was nothing of me in that
boy but the sin. His talent was a source of awe to me. And who
but you could be the maker of such wonders? You soon took him
away from this life on earth, but even now I recall him to mind
without any distress, since there was nothing for me to fear in his
childhood or young adulthood. We took him with us as a companion, as if he were the same age in grace as ourselves, to be trained
in your discipline.

And so we were baptized and all our concerns about our former lives vanished away from us. During the days that followed,
I couldn't get enough of that wonderful sweetness as I meditated
on the depths of your plans for the salvation of the human race.
How freely I wept during your hymns and canticles, how deeply
was I moved by the sweet sounds of your singing church! Those
sounds flooded my ears and the truth poured into my heart, until it
overflowed with complete devotion. Tears ran down my face and

there was joy in those tears . . .

8. You make people to live in harmony together, and so you brought Evodius, a young man from my home town, into our circle. As a civil servant he was converted to you and baptized before us and had resigned from his post to serve you. We stayed together and made the holy intention of living together in the future. Looking for a place where we could serve you most usefully, we decided as a group to return to Africa. And while we were at Ostia on the Tiber, my mother died . . .

Mystical Experience at Ostia [9.10]

10. As the day approached when she was to depart this life—a day you knew, but which we did not—it happened (I believe through your secret arrangements) that she and I stood leaning against a window looking into the garden inside the house where we were staying at Ostia on the Tiber. We were resting there for our sea voyage after our long journey and were chatting pleasantly by ourselves. Forgetting what was behind us and looking out to what was ahead, we were discussing between ourselves, and in the presence of that truth which is you, what the eternal life of the saints would be like . . .

Our conversation reached the conclusion that pleasures of the body, however intense and brilliant they might seem in the radiant light of this physical world, could not be compared to that eternal life, and, indeed, did not even deserve to be mentioned. Then with our minds being lifted up with ardent love for the Selfsame, we raised ourselves still higher, gradually passing beyond all material objects and even the heavens themselves, from which sun, moon, and stars shine upon the earth. And we ascended even higher through inward thought and reflection on the wonders of your works, until we arrived to our own minds. And we went beyond our minds to that land of never-failing plenty where you feed Israel forever with the food of truth. . . .

And while we spoke and panted after it, we just barely touched the edge of it with the entire effort of our hearts. Then, with a sigh, we left behind the first fruits of that spirit and returned to the sounds made by our own mouths, where the spoken word had both a beginning and an end. But how different this from your

Word, our Lord, who abides in himself forever, without becoming old and making all things new!

What we said to one another was something like this: "If the tumult of the flesh were to grow silent for someone, and if the phantasms of earth and water and air were silenced too, and if the heavens themselves were silenced, and if the very soul became silent to itself, by no longer thinking about itself, and if dreams and imaginary revelations were silenced, and if every word and every sign and every transitory thing were silenced for him,...all these things would say, 'We didn't make ourselves; we were made by him who abides forever.'

"If, after having said this, they too should fall silent, having directed our attention to he who made them, then he alone would speak, not through the things that are made, but through himself. And then we would hear his word, not through the tongue of the flesh, or through the voice of an angel, or through a clap of thunder, or some obscure riddle; but we would hear him, who we love in these things, in himself, without the mediation of these things.

"This is how it was when we two, just a moment ago, went beyond ourselves in a flash of thought to touch the eternal wisdom that abides in all things. If this state could last, and that all other visions of a vastly inferior kind could be taken away, leaving on this one to ravage, and absorb, and wrap the beholder in its inward joy, so that his life might forever be like that moment of insight that just passed between us and after which we now sigh—wouldn't this be what is meant by 'Enter into the joy of your Lord.' But when will such a state be? It shall be when we all rise again but are not all changed."

I said something like this, though not exactly in this way and with these words. Yet, Lord, you know that on this day, when we were talking like this, and all the world and all its joys seemed worthless to us, my mother said, "Son, as far as I'm concerned, I now find no pleasure in this life. I don't know what more I have to do here or why I'm still here, since my hopes in this world have already been fulfilled. There was only one reason I wanted to stay here a little longer and that was to see you a Catholic Christian before I died. Now God has fulfilled this wish, for I see you scorning worldly success to be his servant. So, what am I doing here?"

The Death of Monica [9.11 - 13]

11. I can't recall exactly what reply I made to this. Within five days, or not much more, she fell into a fever. One day during her sickness she fainted and lost consciousness. We hurried to her side, and, when she soon regained consciousness, looked at me and [Alypius] as we stood by her, and said, "Where was I?" Then, seeing us struck dumb in our grief, she said, "Here in this place you will bury your mother." I kept silent and fought back my tears. But Alypius, trying to cheer her up, said something about his hopes that she would have the good fortune to die in her own country and not abroad.

When she heard this, she looked at him anxiously and re-proached him, saying, "How absurdly he speaks." Soon after-wards, she said to us, "You may bury this body anywhere you like. Don't worry at all about that. There's only one thing I ask of you—that you both will remember me at the altar of the Lord, wherever you may be." This is what she said, speaking with diffi-culty. Then she fell silent, as the pains of her sickness grew heavi-er . . .

And so, on the ninth day of her illness, at the age of fifty-six, when I was thirty-three, this devout and holy soul was set free from her body.

12. I closed her eyes and a great sadness entered my heart. Tears began to well up in my eyes, but my mind commanded me to hold them back, though the effort was terrible for me. As she breathed her last breath, the boy Adeodatus burst out into loud wails, until he was checked by all of us and grew silent . . . We didn't think it fitting to celebrate a death like hers with tearful wails and protests, since these are the way that people grieve over a miserable death or a death viewed as total extinction. But she didn't die in misery, nor was she completely extinct. We had great confidence about this, because of virtue and sincere faith . . .

When the body was carried away for burial, we went with it, and returned without tears. Not even when we poured out our prayers to you beside the grave for the sacrifice of redemption . . . did I weep. But throughout that day, I mourned secretly, and, in my mental turmoil, I asked you, as well as I could, to heal my sor-row. You wouldn't, and this was because I believe that you were reminding me how strong the bondage of habit is, even to a mind no longer feeding on deceiving words . . .

13. . . . [My mother] didn't desire an expensive burial or to have her body embalmed in spices; nor did she trouble herself about having any special monument or care about a grave in her homeland. She didn't give us any instructions of those kinds. All she wanted was that we remember her at your altar, where she had served without a single day's absence and where she knew your sacrificial victim was made available to all, a victim who erased the debt held against us. He triumphed over that enemy who counts up our sins and looks for whatever he can to charge us with. But he will find nothing to charge against him in whom we have won our victory.

BOOK 10

The Purpose of Confession [10.1-10.4]

1. Let me know you—you who know me. Let me know you as I am known. Strength of my soul enter into it and fit it for yourself, so that you may keep and hold it without spot or blemish. This is my hope and this is why I speak. And, in this hope, my delight is wholesome. As for the other things of this life, the more we weep for them, the less they are to be wept for, and the less we weep for them, the more should they be wept for. For, behold, you love the truth, and one who lives for the truth comes to the light. This is what I desire to do in my heart, before you in my confession and in my writing before many witnesses.

2. But to you, O Lord, the depths of human consciousness are revealed. What could I possibly keep secret from you, even if I were unwilling to confess it to you? I'd be hiding you from myself, but not myself from you. Now when my groaning bears witness to my displeasure towards myself, you shine forth and satisfy my longing—you who are ever beloved and ever desired. And I blush for myself and reject myself, choosing you instead, for it's only through you that I can please either myself or you.

Before you then, Lord, everything that I am is evident, and I have already told of the benefits I have experienced from confessing to you. I don't do this merely through physical words and sounds, but with the words of my soul and with the cry of my thoughts which you well know. When I'm evil, confessing to you is the same as admitting displeasure with myself; but when I'm good, I attribute nothing to myself, because you are the one, Lord, who blesses the righteous . . . Therefore, my God, my confession before you is made both silently and not silently. There is no cry of words, but rather a cry of feeling. If I say anything worthy to other people, you have heard it from me first, and there is nothing worthy that I say that you haven't told me first.

3. Why then do I bother letting others read my confessions? After all, it isn't as though they are going to heal my sickness. Humans are a race extremely inquisitive about other people's lives, but very lazy in improving their own. Why should they want to hear from me about what I am when they don't want to hear from you about what they are? And when they hear me talking about myself, how do they know that I am telling the truth, when no one knows what's going on in another person, except the spirit within? But if they hear about themselves from you, they certainly can't say, "The Lord is lying," for to hear something about oneself from you is to know oneself. Who, then, who has this knowledge says that it's false, unless he's lying? But since love believes all things . . . I will make my confession to you, Lord, so that . . . those whose ears are opened by love may believe me.

Make it clear to me, my innermost healer, what advantage do I gain from doing this? When the confession of my past sins is read and heard . . . this this recitation gladdens the heart, preventing it from from sinking into despair and saying, "I can't do this." Instead the heart is aroused with the love of your mercy and your sweet grace, through which every weak person gains strength and, thanks to this grace of yours, becomes aware of his weakness. It also delights good people to hear about the past sins of those who are now freed of them. They are pleased, not by the sins themselves, but by the fact that they no longer exist.

But, Lord, every day now my conscience makes its confession, relying more on the hope of your mercy than its own innocence. So what advantage is there when I confess through writing to others in your presence, not what I was, but what I still am? Concerning the confessions of my past, I have already seen and spoken about the advantage of that. But there are many people who want to know about what I am now, at the very moment of writing these confessions. This includes both those who know me personally and those who do not—those who have heard either something from me or something about me. None of these individuals have laid their ear against my heart, where I am truly whatever I am. That's why they want to hear from my confession. So, as I make my confession, they want to learn about my innermost self, where neither eye nor ear nor mind can travel. They want to hear and are ready to believe, but will they know? But the love which makes them good tells them that I am not lying about myself in these confessions, and it is the love in them that believes me . . .

4. When confessing not what I was but what I am, the advantage is this: I make my confession not only before you in secret exaltation and trembling, with hidden sorrow infused with hope, but also in the ears of faithful men and women, partners in my joy and sharers in my mortality, my fellow citizens and pilgrims— some who have gone before, some who have gone after me, and all who accompany me through this life . . .

Song of Praise [10.27]

27. Too late did I love you, beauty so ancient yet so new. Too late did I love you! And look: you were within me, but I was outside, searching for you. In my misshapenness, I plunged headlong into the shapely thing you have made. You were there with me, but I was not with you. The beautiful things of this world held me back from you—those things which would have no being had they not been within you. You called and shouted, shattering my deafness; you gleamed and shone, chasing away my blindness; you breathed your fragrance, and I drew in my breath, panting for you; I tasted you, and I am filled with hunger and thirst for you; you touched me, and I am set on fire to attain your peace.

This Life Compared with the Life to Come [10.28]

28. When at last I come to be united with you with my whole self, there will be no more sorrow, no more labors for me, and I will be fully alive, because I will be full of you. You lift up whoever you fill, but since I am not yet full of you, I am still a burden to myself.

There is a conflict over joys in which I should find sorrow and sorrows in which I should find joy. But on which side victory lies, I simply don't know. Have pity on me, Lord, in my anguish . . .

Look, I'm not hiding my wounds. You're the doctor and I'm the sick patient; you're merciful, and I'm in need of mercy. Isn't the life of human beings on earth a trial? Who would choose such troubles and hardships? You command these to be endured, not loved. No one loves what he has to endure, even though he loves to endure. For as much as he may love to endure, he will still prefer that there was nothing for him to have to endure. In adversity, I want prosperity; in prosperous times, I fear adversity. Is there any middle ground between these two where life is not a trial? . . .

Is not the life of human beings on earth an unending trial?

Sexual Temptations [10.29-30]

29. All my hope now rests on your great mercy. Grant us what you command and command what you will. You command us to be continent . . . By continence our scattered remains are bound up and brought back together in the One, whereas before we were scattered among the many. For one loves you too little who loves along with you anything else that he does not love for your sake. O love, ever burning, never extinguished, O charity, my God, set me on fire! You command us to be continent. Grant us what you command and command what you will.

30. Certainly you command me to abstain from the lust of the flesh, the lust of the eyes, and the ambitions of the world. You commanded me to refrain from sleeping with a woman outside of marriage, and, with respect to marriage itself, you advised me to take a better course than the one permitted to me. Because you granted me the power to do this, it was done, even before I became a [priest].

But in my memory . . . images still exist that were fixed there by habit. While I am awake, these images come into my thoughts but have no power. But in my dreams these images not only arouse pleasure, but even illicit consent on my part, making them very much like the acts they represent. These illusionary images have such an effect on my body that they influence me in sleep in a way that they could never have when I'm awake. Aren't I still myself when I'm asleep, Lord? And yet what a great difference there is between myself when I'm asleep and when I'm awake. Where then is my reason, which enables me to resist these temptations when I awake and remains unshaken if such temptations were actually presented to it? Does reason fall asleep with the bodily senses? . . .

Surely, Lord, your hand is strong enough to cure all the sicknesses of my soul, and through your overflowing grace extinguish the lustful impulses of my sleep. I know that you'll increase your gifts in me more and more, so that my soul, rid of the sticky residue of lust, may follow me to you. Then my soul, no longer in opposition to itself, will not, even in dreams, . . . give in to those sordid images which lead to such bodily emissions . . .

Temptations of Eating and Drinking [10.31]

31. There is another evil of the day that I wish I had greater power to control. It's by eating and drinking that we repair the decay of the body, until that time comes when you . . . will kill all physical need with a wonderful fullness . . . But, at the present time, this necessity is pleasant to me and I struggle against that pleasantness to avoid being held captive to it. I wage daily warfare every day by fasting, often succeeding in bringing my body into submission. But the pain I experience in this way is driven out by the pleasure. For hunger and thirst are a kind of pain, which like a fever burn and kill unless relieved by the medicine of nourishment . . .

You've taught me that I should take food in the same way I take medicine. But, while passing from the discomfort of hunger to the satisfaction of having eaten enough, the trap of inordinate desire lies waiting for me in the passage from one to the other. This period of transition is a pleasure, but one which we are forced to go through out of necessity. And while we eat and drink for the sake of health, there is a dangerous kind of pleasure that follows in its footsteps and many times it tries to put itself first, so that I'm actually doing for the sake of pleasure what I claim to be doing for the sake of my health . . .

Confronted by these temptations, I struggle every day against my inordinate desires for food and drink. The problem is that this is not something that I can simply decide to give up once and for all, like I was able to do with sex. And so, the bridle of my throat must be held in a state neither too austere nor too lax. And who, Lord, is there who is not carried away a little beyond the bounds of what is absolutely necessary? Whoever can do this is a great person and let him cry out the greatness of your name. But I'm not that kind of person, because I am a sinful man . . .

Temptations of Sound [10.33]

33. The pleasures [of sound] once held and enthralled me more than they do now, but you broke my bonds and liberated me. Now when I hear sung in a sweet and well-tune voice those tunes into which your word has imparted life, I confess that I feel some peaceful pleasure. I am not completely ensnared by these, since I can free myself from them whenever I wish. While those tunes, when combined with the words that give them life, demand a position of some honor in my heart, it is not always easy for me to strike the right balance with them. Sometimes, I seem to give them more honor than is right. At these times, I may feel that when the sacred words are sung well, our souls are moved to greater religious devotion than when they are not sung quite so well . . . But at other times, I fall into . . . the [opposite] error of being too severe, sometimes wishing that all the pleasant songs adapted from [scripture] be banished from both my ears and those of the Church as well . . .

And so, I'm torn between the dangers of pleasure and the benefits derived from hymns. Though I'm of mixed feelings about this, I'm more inclined to be in support of the practice of singing in Church, so that, through the pleasures of the ear, weaker minds may be aroused to feelings of devotion.

Nevertheless, whenever it happens that singing moves me more than the subject of what is sung, I confess that I am sinning grievously, and I would rather not hear such a singer. Such is my condition. Weep with me and weep for me all of you who have concern for that good from which good actions spring. Those of you who don't share this problem will not be moved by my experience. But you, my Lord God, hear me and look upon me and see. Have mercy and heal me. In your eyes I have become a problem to myself and that is my sickness . . .

The Temptation of Pride [10.36-38]

36. . . . You curbed my pride through fear and tamed my neck by your yoke. And now I wear that yoke and find it light, as you have promised it would be and made it so. In reality it was always light, though I didn't realize it at the time and was afraid to take it upon me.

Is it possible, Lord that this . . . temptation has not ceased to affect me and that it will not cease to affect me during the whole course of this lifetime? This is the temptation to want veneration and affection from others simply for the joy that this provides, which in fact is no true joy at all . . . This is the main reason why I fail to love you with a chaste fear. For you resist the proud and give grace to the humble; you thunder down upon the ambitions of the world and make the foundations of the mountains tremble . . .

37. . . . What should I confess to you, Lord, with regard to this kind of temptation? What can I honestly say except that I take pleasure in praise. But I take more pleasure in the truth than in praise. For if I were given the choice between being mentally enfeebled and wrong on every subject, yet praised by everyone, or standing firm and sure in the truth, yet scorned by everyone, I know which I would choose. And yet I wish that it weren't the case that, when someone praises me, my joy in the good qualities that I possess is increased or that this joy is diminished by criticism. And when I am troubled by this miserable state of mine, I make excuses for myself . . . and this leaves me unsteady.

38. I'm poor and needy, but better off for recognizing this. Groaning inwardly in my dissatisfaction with myself, I seek out your mercy, until that time comes when what is defective in me shall be made right and I am restored to that perfect peace unknown to the proud of heart. But words coming out of the mouth and deeds known to others carry with them the most dangerous temptation from the love of praise, which is like the gathering support for a kind of personal self-glorification. This remains a

temptation for me, even as I condemn this tendency within my-self; for in the act of condemning my own vanity, I run the risk of becoming even more vain . . .

Conclusions [10.40-42]

40. . . . Where have you not walked with me, O Truth, teaching me what to be aware of and what to seek after, as I report to you what I have observed here below and seek out your guidance? . . .

From time to time, you've led me into an inward state of sweet delight quite unlike anything I have ever known before. If I could only remain permanently in this state, it would be an experience quite unlike anything of this world, of this life. But my sad weight makes me fall back into my usual ways, and I am held in their grip. I am held fast and I weep—so much are we weighed down by the burdens of habit. Here I have power to stay, but don't wish to be; there I wish to be but lack the power. In both ways, I'm totally miserable.

41. [And so] I have reflected upon the sickness of my sins and called upon your right hand to help me. With my own wounded heart, I've seen your splendor and have been beaten back. And I called out: "Who can possibly attain that?" . . . You are truth pre-siding over all things. In my greed I didn't want to lose you, but, at the same time, I wanted to possess you with a lie . . . And that's precisely why I lost you: for you will not be possessed together with a lie.

42. Who can I find to reconcile me to you? Should I seek out the aid of angels? What prayer, what sacraments should I use? Many have tried to return to you but, lacking the strength to do it on their own, resort to strange visions and become victims of their own delusions. They deserve this, because they sought you out in arrogance, inflating their chests instead of beating their breasts . . . They sought out a mediator, but it was not the true one, . . . for they were mortal and sinful men.

But in your secret mercy, you showed humanity the true me-diator. You sent him so that by his example, they could learn hu-mility. He is the mediator between God and man—the man Jesus Christ . . . How greatly you loved us, good Father: you didn't even spare your only son, but delivered him over for us sinners . .

. He made us your children rather than your slaves, by being born of you and being servants to us. And so, with good reason my hope is firm in him, for you will cure my diseases through him . . . Otherwise, I'd truly have cause to despair—so many and great are my infirmities. Many and great, indeed! But your medicine is far greater still. We might have thought that your Word was far removed from any union with mankind and we might have despaired, unless he became flesh and dwelt among us . . .

See, Lord, I caste my cares upon you so that I may live. You know my sins and frailties. Teach me and heal me! . . .

Related Readings

Human Happiness
Augustine

The Happy Life was the first work written by Augustine imme-diately following his conversion in 386 A.D. Only a few months after embracing the Christian faith, Augustine had decided to re-treat to a rural estate at Cassiciacum in Northern Italy that had been offered to him by a friend. With him was his mother, Mon-ica, his son, Adeodatus, and a few close friends. Like many of the works that Augustine produced during this period, The Happy Life *is written as a dialogue between himself and his compan-ions. The focus of the work—not surprisingly, given the title—is on happiness and the means by which it is attained.*

Then I asked again, "Do we all wish to be happy?"

I had hardly begun to ask the question, when they all agreed with one voice.

"Does that person," I continued, "seem to be happy who does not have what he wants?"

"Definitely not," they replied.

"So is everyone happy, then, who has what he wants?"

At this my mother responded, "If he wishes for good things and possesses them, then he is happy; but if he wishes for bad things, even if he possess them, he is unhappy."

Smiling at her, I said with joy, "Mother, you have gained true mastery of the stronghold of philosophy. For certainly you were trying to express yourself like Cicero, who similarly dealt with the matter. For, in the *Hortensius*, the work he wrote in praise and defense of philosophy, he stated, "Not philosophers, certainly, but those who are prone to argue, say all are happy who live as they wish. That is not true, for to wish for what is not fitting is the worst kind of misery. It is not quite so misfortunate not to attain what you wish as to wish to acquire what you ought not. For greater evil is brought about through a wicked will than beneficial things through good fortune."

Augustine. *The Happy Life* 1.10-12. Trans. Michael S. Russo, 2011.

At these words, my mother spoke out so enthusiastically that we, forgetting her sex, might have thought that some great man was seated with us. Meanwhile I became aware of the divine source that flowed through her words.

Then Licentius said, "But you ought to tell us what a person should wish for in order to be happy and what sorts of things he should desire."

"Invite me on your birthday," I said, "and I will gladly accept whatever you serve. In this spirit, I beg you to be my guest today and do not ask for what is not prepared."

... I went on to ask, "Do we all now agree that no one can be happy who does not have what he wants and that not everyone who necessarily has what he wants is happy?"

They all expressed their agreement.

"What about this," I asked. "Do you agree that everyone who is not happy is unhappy?"

They did not doubt that.

"Is everyone, then, who does not possess what he wants unhappy?"

They all agreed with this.

"But what ought a man do in order to become happy?" I asked. For perhaps this too is a point that should be served up at our feast, so that the hearty appetite of Licentius might not be neglected. For that which a man wants ought to be obtained when he wishes it.

They all assented to that point.

"Then it must be something," I said, "that must always be enduring, and ought not to depend upon chance nor subject to any misfortunes. For whatever is mortal and transitory we cannot possess when we wish and for as long as we wish."

All were in agreement.

But Trigetius said, "There are many lucky people who possess abundantly and plentifully those things which are delightful, but which are also frail and subject to misfortune. And these lack nothing which they desire."

I replied to him, "Is a person happy who is afraid?"

"It does not seem so," he replied.

"Can a person be without fear, if he can lose what he loves?"

"No he can't," he replied.

"But those things of chance can be lost. Therefore the person who loves and possesses them can never be happy."

He did not argue further.

At this point my mother said, "Even if a person was certain that he would not lose those things, he still would not be satisfied with them. Therefore he is unhappy because he is always wanting."

I replied to her, "Wouldn't that person seem happy to you who has all those things in excess and abundance, but who moderates his desires and enjoys them contentedly, decently, and pleasantly?"

"In that case," she said, "he is happy, then, not because of those things, but due to the moderation of his own mind."

"Extremely well put," I said. "No better answer to this question could have been given by you or anyone else. Let us have no doubt that if anyone desires to be happy, he must obtain for himself that which always endures and which can never be taken away from him through severe misfortune."

"We are in full agreement on that point already," said Trigetius.

"Does God seem to you to be eternal and ever abiding?" I asked.

"That is so obviously true," answered Licentius, "that no further questioning on this point is needed." All the others concurred with pious devotion.

"It follows, therefore, that he who possesses God is happy," I concluded.

As they readily and full-heartedly assented to this, I continued: "the only point now that needs to be inquired about is what sort of person possesses God—for that person certainly will be happy. I'd like to hear your opinions on this matter."

Licentius then volunteered, "That person who lives a good life possesses God."

And Trygetius continued, "That person who does what God wills him to do possesses God."

Lastiduanus also agreed with this opinion.

The boy, who was the youngest of all, said, "That person who does not have an unclean spirit possesses God."

My mother approved all these answers, but especially this

last one.

Navigius remained silent. When I asked him what he thought, he responded that this last opinion was the most pleasing to him. So that Rusticus would not seem to be neglected on a matter of such importance, I asked for his opinion too, for it appeared to me that he was silent, not so much because of deliberation, but because he was shy. He agreed with Trygetius . . .

Original Sin
Augustine

In the City of God, Augustine describes the original state of our first ancestors as one of complete innocence and happiness. From a perverse will, there followed the desire to sin and the resulting just punishment imposed upon the human race by God. This understanding of the fallen nature of mankind colors Augustine's perspective on the behavior of both the infant and child in the Confessions.

The Original Sin of Mankind

God, desiring that the human race . . . might be bound together in harmony and peace by the ties of relationship, was pleased to derive all men from one individual, and created man with such a nature that the members of the race should not have died, had not the two first . . . merited this by their disobedience. For so great was their sin that by it the human nature was altered for the worse, and bondage to sin and inevitable death was passed on to their posterity.

And the kingdom of death so reigned over mankind, that the deserved penalty of sin would have hurled all headlong even into the second death, of which there is no end, had not the undeserved grace of God saved some from that . . .

On Original Peace

But it is fair to ask whether our first parents . . . , before they sinned, experienced in their animal body such emotions as we shall not experience in the spiritual body, when all sin has been purged and finally abolished. For if they did feel them, then how could it be said that they were happy in that famed place of bliss—

Augustine. "City of God." 14.1,10, 11, 13, 15; 22.22. *Nicene and Post Nicene Father*. Vol. 2. Ed. Philip Schaff. Buffalo, NY: Christian Literature Publishing Co., 1887. Translation updated.

Paradise? For can anyone be called absolutely who is affected by fear or grief?

And what could those persons fear or suffer in such affluence of blessings, where neither death nor sickness was feared, and where nothing was wanting which a good will could desire, and nothing present which could interrupt man's mental or bodily enjoyment? Their love to God was unclouded, and their mutual affection was that of faithful and sincere marriage; and from this love flowed a wonderful delight, because they always enjoyed what was loved. Their avoidance of sin was tranquil, and, so long as it was maintained, no other ill at all could invade them and bring sorrow . . .

Happy, then, were these our first parents, who were agitated by neither mental perturbations, nor annoyed by bodily discomforts. So happy too would the whole human race have been had they not introduced that evil which they have transmitted to their posterity and had none of their descendants committed sins worthy of damnation. This original blessedness, moreover, would have continued until . . . the number of the predestined saints should have been completed. There would then have been bestowed that bliss which is enjoyed by the most blessed angels. In this state there would have been a secure assurance that no one would sin and no one die. And so would the saints have lived, with no taste of labor, pain, or death, as now they shall live in the resurrection, after they have endured all these things . . .

The Fall of Humankind

Thus, as it is written in Scripture, God made man upright, and consequently with a good will. For if he had not had a good will, he could not have been upright. The good will, then, is the work of God; for God created him with it. But the first evil will, which preceded all man's evil acts, was rather a kind of falling away from the work of God to its own works than any positive work. And therefore the acts resulting were evil, not having God, but the will itself for their end. And so that the will or the man himself, so far as his will is bad, was, as it were, the evil tree bringing forth evil fruit . . .

The Evil Will as the Cause of the First Sin

Our first parents fell into open disobedience because already they were secretly corrupted. For the evil act would never have happened had not an evil will preceded it. And what is the origin of our evil will but pride? For "pride is the beginning of sin." And what is pride but the craving for undue exaltation? And this is undue exaltation, when the soul abandons God, whom it ought to desire as its end, and becomes a kind of end to itself. This happens when it becomes its own satisfaction. And it does so when it falls away from that unchangeable good which ought to satisfy it more than itself. This falling away is spontaneous.

If the will had remained steadfast in the love of that higher and changeless good by which it was illumined to intelligence and kindled into love, it would not have turned away to find satisfaction in itself, and so would not have become so cold and darkened. The woman would not have believed the serpent spoke the truth, nor would the man have preferred the request of his wife to the command of God, nor have supposed that it was a minor transgression to cling to the partner of his life even in a partnership of sin . . .

The Punishment that Follows the Fall

Man despised the authority of God, who had created him, who had made him in his own image, who had set him above the other animals, who had placed him in Paradise, who had enriched him with abundance of every kind, who had laid upon him neither many, nor great, nor difficult commandments, but gave him simple rules to obey . . . to support him in his wholesome obedience. It was, therefore, right that condemnation followed . . . And just as man in his pride had sought to be his own satisfaction, God in his justice abandoned him to himself, not to live in the absolute independence he affected, but instead of the liberty he desired. He was to live dissatisfied with himself in a hard and miserable bondage . . . , doomed in spite of himself to die in body as he had willingly become dead in spirit, condemned even to eternal death (had not the grace of God delivered him) because he had forsaken eternal life . . .

The Effects of the Fall on Mankind

As for the first origin of mankind, this life of ours bears witness to the fact that the descendants of the first man have come under condemnation. Is not this proved by the profound and dreadful ignorance which produces all the errors that ensnare the children of Adam, and from which no man can be rescued without toil, pain, and fear? Is it not proved by his love of so many vain and harmful things, which produces gnawing cares, disquiet, griefs, fears, wild joys, quarrels, lawsuits, wars, treasons, angers, hatreds, deceit, flattery, fraud, theft, robbery, faithlessness, pride, ambition, envy, murders,parricides, cruelty, ferocity, wickedness, luxury, insolence, impudence, shamelessness, fornications, adulteries, incest, unnatural vice in both sexes too shameful to mention, sacrileges, heresies, blasphemies, perjuries, oppression of the innocent, slanders, plots, lies, false witness, unrighteous judgments, violence, robbery, and all other evils deeds . . . that afflict the lives of human beings?

These are indeed the crimes of wicked men, yet they spring from that root of error and misplaced love which is born with every son of Adam. For who is there that has not observed the profound ignorance (which manifests itself even in infancy) and the flood of foolish desires (beginning in boyhood) which accompanies man in life, such that, if he left to live as he pleased, and to do whatever he pleased, he would plunge into all, or certainly into many of those crimes and iniquities which I mentioned, and others still which I have not mentioned?

But God does not wholly desert those whom he condemns, nor does he in his anger withhold his tender mercy. And so the human race is restrained by law and instruction, which keep guard against the ignorance that besets us, and oppose the assaults of vice, but are themselves full of labor and sorrow. For what is the purpose of those many threats which are used to restrain the folly of children? What is the purpose of the teacher, the master, the stick, the strap, the cane, and all other types of discipline? As sacred Scripture teaches a child must be beaten on the sides to prevent him from becoming stubborn, untamable, and eventually impossible to discipline at all.

What is the point of all these punishments, if not to over-come ignorance and to restrain evil desires — these evils with which we come into the world? Why is it that it is so hard to learn, but so easy to forget? . . . Doesn't this show that state into which our corrupted nature has sunken and how much help it needs to be delivered? Inactivity, sloth, laziness, and negligence are vic-es which make us shun all labor, since labor, though useful, is itself a punishment.

But, besides the punishments of childhood, without which there would be no learning, . . . there are pains which trouble not only the unrighteous, but are part of the condition of all man-kind . . . What fear and what grief are caused by bereavement and mourning, by losses and condemnations, by fraud and falsehood, by false suspicions, and all the crimes and wicked deeds of other men? For at their hands we suffer robbery, captivity, chains, im-prisonment, exile, torture, mutilation, loss of sight, the violation of chastity to satisfy the lust of the oppressor, and many other dreadful evils.

What numberless casualties threaten our bodies from without — from extremes of heat and cold, storms, floods, inundations, lightning, thunder, hail, earthquakes, houses falling . . . [and] from countless poisons in fruits, water, air, animals; from the painful or even deadly bites of wild animals.

What disasters are suffered by those who travel by land or sea! What man can go out of his own house without being exposed on all hands to unforeseen accidents? Returning home sound in limb, he slips on his own doorstep, breaks his leg, and never recovers. What can seem safer than a man sitting in his chair? And yet, the priest Eli fell from his, and broke his neck. How many accidents do farmers, or rather all men, fear that the crops may suffer from the weather, or the soil, or the ravages of destructive animals? . . .

As to bodily diseases, they are so numerous that they cannot all be contained even in medical books. And in very many, or almost all of them, the cures and remedies are themselves tortures, so that people are rescued from a painful disease by a painful cure . . .

From this kind of hell on earth, there is no escape, except through the grace of the Savior Christ, our God and Lord . . . , a grace which aids good men in the midst of their present miseries,

so that they are able to endure them with a courage proportioned
to their faith.

The Right Order of Loves

Augustine

In The Happy Life, *Augustine and his companions agree that those who possess God must be happy.* In Christian Doctrine, *which was written a decade later, Augustine spells out what it means to possess God by making a distinction between two forms of love: use (*uti*) and enjoyment (*frui*). Augustine argues that God alone is to be enjoyed—that is, loved for his own sake—while all other things, including ourselves and others, are to be loved for the sake of God. This is not merely an academic issue for Augustine since he believes that getting this distinction right is the key to our ultimate happiness.*

Use and Enjoyment

There are some things . . . which are to be enjoyed, others which are to be used, others still which enjoy and use. Those things which are objects of enjoyment make us happy. Those things which are objects of use assist, and (so to speak) support us in our efforts after happiness, so that we can attain the things that make us happy and rest in them. We ourselves, again, who enjoy and use these things, being placed among both kinds of objects, if we set ourselves to enjoy those which we ought to use, are hindered in our course, and sometimes even led away from it; so that, getting entangled in the love of lower gratifications, we lag behind in, or even altogether turn back from, the pursuit of the real and proper objects of enjoyment.

For to enjoy a thing is to rest with satisfaction in it for its own sake. To use, on the other hand, is to employ whatever means are at one's disposal to obtain what one desires, if it is a proper object of desire; for an unlawful use ought rather to be called an abuse. Suppose, then, we were wanderers in a strange country, and could not live happily away from our fatherland, and that we felt wretched in our wandering, and wishing to put an end to

Augustine. "Christian Doctrine." 1.3-4; 20-21; 28. Trans. J.F. Shaw. *Nicene and Post Nicene Fathers*. Vol. 1. Edinburgh: T and T Clark, 1886.

our misery, determined to return home. We find, however, that we must make use of some mode of conveyance, either by land or water, in order to reach that fatherland where our enjoyment is to commence. But the beauty of the country through which we pass, and the very pleasure of the motion, charm our hearts, and turning these things which we ought to use into objects of enjoyment, we become unwilling to hasten the end of our journey; and becoming engrossed in a factitious delight, our thoughts are diverted from that home whose delights would make us truly happy.

Such is a picture of our condition in this life of mortality. We have wandered far from God; and if we wish to return to our Father's home, this world must be used, not enjoyed, that so the invisible things of God may be clearly seen, being understood by the things that are made—that is, that by means of what is material and temporary we may lay hold upon that which is spiritual and eternal.

God Alone to Be Enjoyed

Among all these things, then, those only are the true objects of enjoyment which we have spoken of as eternal and unchangeable. The rest are for use, that we may be able to arrive at the full enjoyment of the former. We, however, who enjoy and use other things are things ourselves. For a great thing truly is man, made after the image and similitude of God, not as respects the mortal body in which he is clothed, but as respects the rational soul by which he is exalted in honor above the beasts.

And so it becomes an important question, whether men ought to enjoy, or to use, themselves, or to do both. For we are commanded to love one another: but it is a question whether man is to be loved by man for his own sake, or for the sake of something else. If it is for his own sake, we enjoy him; if it is for the sake of something else, we use him. It seems to me, then, that he is to be loved for the sake of something else. For if a thing is to be loved for its own sake, then in the enjoyment of it consists a happy life, the hope of which at least, if not yet the reality, is our comfort in the present time. But a curse is pronounced on him who places his hope in man.

Neither ought any one to have joy in himself, if you look at the matter clearly, because no one ought to love even himself for his own sake, but for the sake of Him who is the true object of enjoyment. For a man is never in so good a state as when his whole life is a journey towards the unchangeable life, and his affections are entirely fixed upon that. If, however, he loves himself for his own sake, he does not look at himself in relation to God, but turns his mind in upon himself, and so is not occupied with anything that is unchangeable. And thus he does not enjoy himself at his best, because he is better when his mind is fully fixed upon, and his affections wrapped up in, the unchangeable good, than when he turns from that to enjoy even himself.

Therefore if you ought not to love even yourself for your own sake, but for His in whom your love finds its most worthy object, no other man has a right to be angry if you love him too for God's sake. For this is the law of love that has been laid down by Divine authority: "You shall love thy neighbor as yourself;" but, "You shall love God with all your heart, and with all your soul, and with all your mind:" so that you are to concentrate all your thoughts, your whole life and your whole intelligence upon Him from whom you derive all that you bring. For when He says, "With all your heart, and with all your soul, and with all your mind," He means that no part of our life is to be unoccupied, and to afford room, as it were, for the wish to enjoy some other object, but that whatever else may suggest itself to us as an object worthy of love is to be borne into the same channel in which the whole current of our affections flows.

Whoever, then, loves his neighbor aright, ought to urge upon him that he too should love God with his whole heart, and soul, and mind. For in this way, loving his neighbor as himself, a man turns the whole current of his love both for himself and his neighbor into the channel of the love of God, which suffers no stream to be drawn off from itself by whose diversion its own volume would be diminished.

The Right Order of Love

Now he is a man of just and holy life who forms an unprejudiced estimate of things, and keeps his affections also under strict control, so that he neither loves what he ought not to love, nor fails to love what he ought to love, nor loves that more which ought to be loved less, nor loves that equally which ought to be loved either less or more, nor loves that less or more which ought to be loved equally. No sinner is to be loved as a sinner; and every man is to be loved as a man for God's sake; but God is to be loved for His own sake. And if God is to be loved more than any man, each man ought to love God more than himself. Likewise we ought to love another man better than our own body, because all things are to be loved in reference to God, and another man can have fellowship with us in the enjoyment of God, whereas our body cannot; for the body only lives through the soul, and it is by the soul that we enjoy God.

Plundering the Gold of the Egyptians
Augustine

Just as the Israelites plundered the gold of the Egyptians as they were led out of their captivity in that country, so does Augustine argue that pagan wisdom may be made use of by Christians in their quest for salvation. Of course, he also maintains that there is nothing of value in the teachings of even the wisest pagans that can't be found in scripture.

. . . If those who are called philosophers, and especially the Platonists, have said anything that is true and in harmony with our faith, not only should we not be afraid of them, but we should even claim it for our own use from those who have unlawfully taken possession of it. For, the Egyptians had not only the idols and heavy burdens which the people of Israel hated and fled from, but also vessels and ornaments of gold and silver, and garments, which the same people, when going out of Egypt, appropriated to themselves and put to better use. They did this, not on their own authority, but by the command of God, with the Egyptians themselves, in their ignorance, providing them with things which they themselves were not making a good use of.

In the same way all branches of heathen learning have, not only false and superstitious fictions and heavy burdens of unnecessary labor, which every one of us ought to abhor and shun as we go out under the leadership of Christ from the fellowship of the heathen; but their teachings also contain liberal instructions which are better adapted to the use of the truth as well as a number of excellent moral principles. And some truths are found among them even with respect to the worship of the one, true God.

Now all these are their gold and silver, which they did not create themselves, but dug out of the mines of God's providence which are everywhere to be found. As they perversely and un-

Augustine. "Christine Doctrine" 2.60-63. Trans. J.F. Shaw. *Nicene and Post Nicene Fathers*. Vol. 1. Edinburgh: T and T Clark, 1886. Translation updated.

lawfully use it in the service of evil, the Christian, when he separates himself in spirit from the miserable fellowship of these men, ought to take away from them, and to devote to their proper use in preaching the gospel. Their garments, also—that is, human institutions such as are adapted to that intercourse with men which is indispensable in this life—we must take and turn to a Christian use.

And what else have many good and faithful men among our brethren done? Do we not see with what a quantity of gold and silver and garments [notable Christian teachers of the past brought out with them], not to speak of living men! How much Greeks out of number have borrowed! And prior to all these, that most faithful servant of God, Moses, had done the same thing; for of him it is written that he was learned in all the wisdom of the Egyptians. And to none of all these would heathen superstition (especially in those times when, kicking against the yoke of Christ, it was persecuting the Christians) have ever furnished branches of knowledge it held useful, if it had suspected they were about to turn them to the use of worshiping the One God, and thereby overturning the vain worship of idols. But they gave their gold and their silver and their garments to the people of God as they were going out of Egypt, not knowing how the things they gave would be turned to the service of Christ. For what was done at the time of the exodus was no doubt a type prefiguring what happens now. And this I say without prejudice to any other interpretation that may be as good, or better . . .

But just as poor as the store of gold and silver and garments which the people of Israel brought with them out of Egypt was in comparison with the riches which they afterwards attained at Jerusalem, and which reached their height in the reign of King Solomon, so poor is all the useful knowledge which is gathered from the books of the heathen when compared with the knowledge of Holy Scripture, For whatever man may have learnt from other sources, if it is hurtful, it is there condemned; if it is useful, it is therein contained. And while every man may find there everything useful that he has learned elsewhere, he will find there in much greater abundance things that are to be found nowhere else but can be learnt only in the wonderful sublimity and wonderful simplicity of the Scriptures.

The Goodness of Creation
Augustine

In the following passage from On the Nature of the Good, *Augustine describes what would come to be known as the "great chain of being," a hierarchical structuring of all reality that would influence Medieval metaphysics. God sits at the top of this chain and represents the perfection of goodness. Because all other things in the created realm flow out from him, his goodness is also present in them. This worldview provided Augustine with an alternative to Manichaean dualism.*

The highest good, than which there is no higher, is God, and consequently He is unchangeable good, hence truly eternal and truly immortal. All other good things are only from Him, not of Him. For what is of Him, is Himself. And consequently if He alone is unchangeable, all things that He has made, because He has made them out of nothing, are changeable. For He is so omnipotent, that even out of nothing, that is out of what is absolutely non-existent, He is able to make good things both great and small, both celestial and terrestrial, both spiritual and corporeal. But because He is also just, He has not put those things that He has made out of nothing on an equality with that which He begot out of Himself.

Because, therefore, no good things whether great or small, through whatever gradations of things, can exist except from God; but since every nature, so far as it is nature, is good, it follows that no nature can exist save from the most high and true God: because all things even not in the highest degree good, but related to the highest good, and again, because all good things, even those of most recent origin, which are far from the highest good, can have their existence only from the highest good.

Therefore every spirit, though subject to change, and every corporeal entity, is from God, and all this, having been made, is nature. For every nature is either spirit or body. Unchangeable spirit

Augustine "On the Nature of the Good." 1-3. Trans. Albert H. Newman. *Nicene and Post-Nicene Fathers*. Vol. 4. Edited by Philip Schaff. Buffalo, NY: Christian Literature Publishing Co., 1887.

is God, changeable spirit, having been made, is nature, but is better than body; but body is not spirit, unless when the wind, because it is invisible to us and yet its power is felt as something not inconsiderable, is in a certain sense called spirit . . .

For we Catholic Christians worship God, from whom are all good things whether great or small; from whom is all measure great or small; from whom is all form great or small; from whom is all order great or small. For all things in proportion as they are better measured, formed, and ordered, are assuredly good in a higher degree; but in proportion as they are measured, formed, and ordered in an inferior degree, are they the less good. These three things, therefore, measure, form, and order—not to speak of innumerable other things that are shown to pertain to these three—these three things, therefore, measure, form, order, are as it were generic goods in things made by God, whether in spirit or in body.

God is, therefore, above every measure of the creature, above every form, above every order, nor is He above by local spaces, but by ineffable and singular potency, from whom is every measure, every form, every order. These three things, where they are great, are great goods, where they are small, are small goods; where they are absent, there is no good. And again where these things are great, there are great natures, where they are small, there are small natures, where they are absent, there is no nature. Therefore all nature is good.

Evil as a Corruption of the Good
Augustine

In a direct repudiation of Manichaean doctrine, Augustine argues that evil lacks any independent existence. Instead, he maintains that only good exists and that evil is simply a corruption (or privation) of some essentially good thing.

All of nature, therefore, is good, since the Creator of all nature is supremely good. But nature is not supremely and immutably good as is the Creator of it. Thus, the good in created things can be diminished and increased. For good to be diminished is evil; still, however much it is diminished, something must remain of its original nature as long as it exists at all. For no matter what kind or however insignificant a thing may be, the good which is its "nature" cannot be destroyed without the thing itself being destroyed.

There is good reason, therefore, to praise an uncorrupted thing, and if it were indeed an incorruptible thing which could not be destroyed, it would certainly be all the more worthy of praise. When, however, a thing is corrupted, its corruption is an evil because it is, by just so much, a privation of the good. Where there is no privation of the good, there is no evil. Where there is evil, there is a corresponding diminution of the good. As long, then, as a thing is being corrupted, there is good in it of which it is being deprived; and in this process, if something of its being remains that cannot be further corrupted, this will then be an incorruptible entity, and to this great good it will have come through the process of corruption. But even if the corruption is not halted, it still does not cease having some good of which it cannot be further deprived.

If, however, the corruption comes to be total and entire, there is no good left either, because it is no longer an entity at all. So, corruption cannot consume the good without also consuming the

Augustine. "Enchiridion." 12-14. Trans. J.F. Shaw. *Nicene and Post-Nicene Fathers*. Vol. 3. Edited by Philip Schaff. Buffalo, NY: Christian Literature Publishing Co., 1887. Translation updated.

thing itself. Every actual entity is therefore good; a greater good if it cannot be corrupted, a lesser good if it can be. Yet only the foolish and unknowing can deny that it is still good even when corrupted. Whenever a thing is consumed by corruption, not even the corruption remains, for it is nothing in itself, having no subsistent being in which to exist.

From this it follows that there is nothing to be called evil if there is nothing good. A good that wholly lacks an evil aspect is entirely good. Where there is some evil in a thing, its good is defective or subject to defect. Thus there can be no evil where there is no good. This leads us to a surprising conclusion: that, since every being, in so far as it is a being, is good, if we then say that a defective thing is bad, it would seem to mean that we are saying that what is evil is good, that only what is good is ever evil and that there is no evil apart from something good. This is because every actual entity is good.

Nothing evil exists *in itself,* but only as an evil aspect of some actual entity. Therefore, there can be nothing evil except something good. Absurd as this sounds, nevertheless the logical connections of the argument compel us to it as inevitable . . .

Now, if a man is something good because he is an entity, what, then, is a bad man except an evil good? When, however, we distinguish between these two concepts, we find that the bad man is not bad because he is a man, nor is he good because he is wicked. Rather, he is a good entity in so far as he is a man, evil in so far as he is wicked . . . Thus, every entity, even if it is a defective one, in so far as it is an entity, is good. In so far as it is defective, it is evil.

Actually, then, in these two contraries we call evil and good, the rule of the logicians fails to apply. No weather is both dark and bright at the same time; no food or drink is both sweet and sour at the same time; no body is, at the same time and place, both white and black, nor deformed and well-formed at the same time. This principle is found to apply in almost all disjunctions: two contraries cannot coexist in a single thing. Nevertheless, while no one maintains that good and evil are not contraries, they can not only coexist, but the evil cannot exist at all without the good, or in a thing that is not a good. On the other hand, the good can exist without evil. For a man or an angel could exist and yet not be wicked, whereas there cannot be wickedness except in a man or an angel. It is good to be a man, good to be an angel; but evil to be wicked. These two contraries are thus coexistent, so that if there were no good in what is evil, then the evil simply could not be, since it can have no mode in which to exist, nor any source from which corruption springs, unless it be something corruptible.

Unless this something is good, it cannot be corrupted, because corruption is nothing more than the deprivation of the good. Evils, therefore, have their source in the good, and unless they are parasitic on something good, they are not anything at all. There is no other source whence an evil thing can come to be. If this is the case, then, in so far as a thing is an entity, it is unquestionably good. If it is an incorruptible entity, it is a great good. But even if it is a corruptible entity, it still has no mode of existence except as an aspect of something that is good. Only by corrupting something good can corruption inflict injury.

Human Freedom and Punishment
Augustine

The text, On the Freedom of the Will, *is significant because it was written over a period of several years during which Augustine's views on this human freedom would change dramatically. Books I and II, which were written not long after Augustine's conversion, are fairly optimistic about man's freedom to choose the good and avoid evil. Book III, however, was written later as Augustine began to absorb the insights of St. Paul about original sin and the slavery of habit. In this text, we can see Augustine beginning to come to grips with the question of how human beings can still be responsible for sins they do not willingly commit and which are the penalty for sins committed by our original ancestors.*

BOOK I

1. Is God the Cause of Evil?

EVODIUS: Will you please tell me whether or not God is the cause of evil.

AUGUSTINE: I'll tell you, if you explain what kind of evil you're talking about. We typically speak of "evil" in two ways: first, the evil that someone has done, and, second, the evil someone has suffered.

EVODIUS: I want to know about both kinds.

AUGUSTINE: Well, if you believe that God is good (and it is wrong to think otherwise) he does not do evil. On the other hand, if we believe that God is just (and it is blasphemous to deny this), then we must also believe that he gives rewards to the good and punishes the wicked—punishments which naturally are evils to those who suffer them. So, if no one is punished unjustly (and we must believe this if we hold that the world is governed by divine providence), then God is the cause of the evil that human beings

Augustine. *On the Freedom of the Will* 1.1; 3.4, 18, 19. Trans. Michael S. Russo (2019).

suffer, but not the evil that human beings do. Therefore if no one is punished unjustly (and this we must believe, since we believe that the universe is governed by divine providence), then God is not the author of the evil a man does though he is the author of the evil a man suffers.

EVODIUS: Then is there some other cause of that kind of evil that we don't attribute to God?

AUGUSTINE: Of course there is, for evil could not occur without a cause But if you ask what the cause is, I can't tell you, since there is no single cause. Every individual is the cause of his or her own evil deeds. If you doubt this, then consider what I just said—namely, that evil deeds are punished by God's justice. They would not be punished justly had they not been performed voluntarily . . .

BOOK III

4. The Will Must Be Free

AUGUSTINE: I'm sure you'll remember that in our previous discussion we agreed that nothing can make the mind a slave to sinful desire except its own will. It cannot be forced to do so by anything superior or equal to it, since that would be unjust, and it could not be forced by anything inferior to it, since an inferior thing would not have the power to compel it. The only other possibility, then, is that the movement by which the will turns from the enjoyment of the Creator to the enjoyment of lesser created things belongs to the will itself. So if that movement deserves blame, . . . then it is not natural, but voluntary.

Such a movement is similar to the downward falling of a stone in that the movement of a stone belongs to itself just as the movement of the mind belongs to itself. But it is dissimilar in that the stone doesn't have the power to stop its downward movement, whereas, the mind is not moved to abandon higher things and love inferior things, unless it wills to do so. Thus, the movement of a stone is natural, but the movement of the mind is voluntary. If someone were to say that a soul "sins" because it is carried downward by its weight, I wouldn't just say that he is a as stupid as a stone, but that he's simply insane....

EVODIUS: I see . . . that what you're saying is true. There's nothing I feel so strongly and intimately as that I have a will by which I am moved to enjoy something. I know nothing I can call more my own than the will by which I accept or reject things. So, if I use it to do evil, who should that evil be attributed to if not myself? Since a good God made me, I can't do any good except by my will, and it is clear that he gave me my will for that purpose. And, if the movement of that will was not voluntary, and not in our power, a person would not be deserving praise when he turned to higher things or blamed for turning to lower things....

18. The Recognition of Inherited Sin

AUGUSTINE: . . . Nonetheless, there are some acts which are done out of ignorance that are condemned and deserving of correction, as we read in sacred scripture where St. Paul says, "I obtained mercy, because I did it out of ignorance. And the prophet says, "Remember not the sins of my youth and my ignorance." Even things done out of necessity are blameworthy when someone wants to act rightly but cannot. This is the meaning of the following passages from scripture: "I do not do the good that I will; but the evil that I hate, that I do." "To will the good is present to me, but I find no way to do it." "The flesh lusts against the spirit and the spirit against the flesh; for they war against each other, so that you do not do what you will."

All these are the result of the sentence of death passed upon human beings, for if they were not penalties, but part of our nature, they wouldn't be sins . . . Who could doubt that this is a penalty? But every just penalty is a penalty for sin and is called a "punishment" . . . It follows, therefore, that this just penalty is the result of the condemnation of human beings.

It shouldn't be any wonder that, because of our ignorance, we lack the free choice of the will to act rightly, or that we see what is right and will to do it, but can't because of the resistance of carnal habits, which has grown almost as strong as nature, because of the unruliness of our mortal inheritance. Indeed, it is completely just that we should lose what we were unwilling to use properly, since we could without difficulty have used it had we so willed to do so. Thus, we who knew what was right but didn't do it lost the knowledge of what was right. And we who had the power to act rightly, but didn't do so, lost that power, even when we had the will.

There really are two penalties that afflict a sinful soul—ignorance and difficulty. Due to ignorance, the soul is warped by error; due to difficulty, our lives are afflicted by torment. But to accept falsehood as truth, so that one errs against his will and to be unable to refrain from lust, because of the pain involved in breaking away from carnal desires—these two things are not part of the nature that human beings as originally created, but are the penalty of one who has been condemned. When we speak of the free will to do what is right, we are speaking of the freedom with which human beings were originally made.

19. Why This Penalty is Just

Now, let's deal with that question so often raised by those ready to lay the blame for sinning on anything but themselves: "If it was Adam and Eve who sinned, what did we poor people do to be born with the blindness of ignorance and the torment of difficulties? Why should we first wander about not knowing what to do, falling into error, and then, when the precepts of justice begin to be revealed to us, we will to do the right thing, but are prevented from doing do, because of carnal desire?"

My response to them is brief: Keep quiet and stop muttering against God. Perhaps their complaints would be justified if there was no one who ever triumphed over error and inordinate desire. But there is one present everywhere, who in many ways through his creation that serves him as Lord, calls out to those who have gone astray, teaches those who believe, comforts the hopeful, encourages the persistent, helps the struggling, and hears those who pray.

You aren't at fault for acting out of ignorance against your will, but rather because you don't ask about what you don't know. You're not at fault because you don't bind up your own wounds, but because you reject the one willing to heal you. These are your personal sins. A person . . . must humbly confess his weakness, so that God, who knows neither error nor difficulty, may come to his aid.

When anyone out of ignorance doesn't do what is right or cannot do what he rightly will to do, these actions are called sins, because they have their origin in the first sin of free will. These later sins are the consequences of that first sin.... For we use the word "sin," not only for sin in the strict sense of the word—namely, that which is performed knowingly and through free will—but also that which now necessarily follows from the punishment of those sins.

Similarly, we also talk about "nature," not only in the sense of that nature in which human beings were first created, faultless in their kind, but also that nature—mortal, ignorant and enslaved by the flesh—of those of us who were born as a result of the penalty for condemnation. This latter sense is what St. Paul refers to when he says, "We were born by nature children of wrath, as were the others."

The Ascent Towards the Good
Plotinus

In Book 7 of the Confessions, *Augustine describes how after reading "the books of the Platonists," he was inspired to "enter into [his] innermost self."[7.10] The Neo-Platonists that Augustine probably encountered at this time were Plotinus and Porphyry, both of whom he almost certainly read in the Latin translation of Marius Victorinus. The following is Plotinus' account of the ascent of the soul to the Good, which may have influenced Augustine's own account in Book 7.*

Therefore we must ascend again towards the Good, the desired of every Soul. Anyone that has seen This, knows what I intend when I say that it is beautiful. Even the desire of it is to be desired as a good. To attain it is for those that will take the upward path, who will set all their forces towards it, who will divest themselves of all that we have put on in our descent so, to those that approach the Holy Celebrations of the Mysteries, there are appointed purifications and the laying aside of the garments worn before, and the entry in nakedness—until, passing, on the upward way, all that is other than the God, each in the solitude of himself shall behold that solitary dwelling Existence, the Apart, the Unmingled, the Pure, that from Which all things depend, for Which all look and live and act and know, the Source of Life and of Intellection and of Being.

And one that shall know this vision—with what passion of love shall he not be seized, with what pang of desire, what longing to be molten into one with This, what wondering delight! If he that has never seen this Being must hunger for It as for all his welfare, he that has known must love and reverence It as the very Beauty; he will be flooded with awe and gladness, stricken by a salutary terror; he loves with a veritable love, with sharp desire; all other loves than this he must despise, and disdain all that once seemed fair.

Plotinus. *The Six Enneads* 1.6. Trans. Stephen MacKenna. London: Medici Society, 1917. Translation updated.

This, indeed, is the mood even of those who, having witnessed the manifestation of Gods or Supernatural Beings, can never again feel the old delight in the comeliness of material forms: what then are we to think of one that contemplates Absolute Beauty in Its essential integrity, no accumulation of flesh and matter, no dweller on earth or in the heavens- so perfect Its purity- far above all such things in that they are non-essential, composite, not primal but descending from This?

Beholding this Being, . . . resting, rapt, in the vision and possession of so lofty a loveliness, growing to Its likeness, what Beauty can the soul yet lack? For This, the Beauty supreme, the absolute, and the primal, fashions Its lovers to Beauty and makes them also worthy of love.

And for This, the sternest and the uttermost combat is set before the Souls; all our labor is for This, lest we be left without part in this noblest vision, which to attain is to be blessed in the blissful sight, which to fail of is to fail utterly.

For not he that has failed of the joy that is in color or in visible forms, not he that has failed of power or of honors or of kingdom has failed, but only he that has failed of only This, for Whose winning he should renounce kingdoms and command over earth and ocean and sky, if only, spurning the world of sense from beneath his feet, and straining to This, he may see . . .

But what must we do? How lies the path? How come to vision of the inaccessible Beauty, dwelling as if in consecrated precincts, apart from the common ways where all may see, even the profane?

He that has the strength, let him arise and withdraw into himself, foregoing all that is known by the eyes, turning away for ever from the material beauty that once made his joy. When he perceives those shapes of grace that show in body, let him not pursue: he must know them for copies, vestiges, shadows, and hasten away towards That they tell of. For if anyone follow what is like a beautiful shape playing over water- is there not a myth telling in symbol of such a dupe, how he sank into the depths of the current and was swept away to nothingness? So too, one that is held by material beauty and will not break free shall be precipitated, not in body but in Soul, down to the dark depths loathed of the Intellective-Being, where, blind even in the Lower-World, he shall have commerce only with shadows, there as here.

"Let us flee then to the beloved Fatherland": this is the sound-
est counsel. But what is this flight? How are we to gain the open
sea? For Odysseus is surely a parable to us when he commands
the flight from the sorceries of Circe or Calypso—not content to
linger for all the pleasure offered to his eyes and all the delight of
sense filling his days.

The Fatherland to us is There whence we have come, and
There is The Father.

What then is our course, what the manner of our flight? This
is not a journey for the feet; the feet bring us only from land to
land; nor need you think of coach or ship to carry you away; all
this order of things you must set aside and refuse to see: you must
close the eyes and call instead upon another vision which is to be
waked within you, a vision, the birth-right of all, which few turn
to use. (1.6.7)

And this inner vision, what is its operation?

Newly awakened it is all too feeble to bear the ultimate splendor. Therefore the Soul must be trained—to the habit of remark-
ing, first, all noble pursuits, then the works of beauty produced
not by the labor of the arts but by the virtue of men known for
their goodness: lastly, you must search the souls of those that have
shaped these beautiful forms.

But how are you to see into a virtuous soul and know its loveliness?

Withdraw into yourself and look. And if you do not find yourself beautiful yet, act as does the creator of a statue that is to be
made beautiful: he cuts away here, he smooths there, he makes
this line lighter, this other purer, until a lovely face has grown
upon his work. So do you also: cut away all that is excessive,
straighten all that is crooked, bring light to all that is overcast,
labor to make all one glow of beauty and never cease chiseling
your statue, until there shall shine out on you from it the godlike
splendor of virtue, until you shall see the perfect goodness surely
established in the stainless shrine.

When you know that you have become this perfect work, when
you are self-gathered in the purity of your being, nothing now re-
maining that can shatter that inner unity, nothing from without

clinging to the authentic man, when you find yourself wholly true to your essential nature, wholly that only veritable Light which is not measured by space, not narrowed to any circumscribed form nor again diffused as a thing void of term, but ever unmeasurable as something greater than all measure and more than all quantity-when you perceive that you have grown to this, you are now become very vision: now call up all your confidence, strike forward yet a step—you need a guide no longer—strain, and see.

This is the only eye that sees the mighty Beauty. If the eye that adventures the vision be dimmed by vice, impure, or weak, and unable in its cowardly blenching to see the uttermost brightness, then it sees nothing even though another point to what lies plain to sight before it. To any vision must be brought an eye adapted to what is to be seen, and having some likeness to it. Never did eye see the sun unless it had first become sunlike, and never can the soul have vision of the First Beauty unless itself be beautiful.

Therefore, first let each become godlike and each beautiful who cares to see God and Beauty. So, mounting, the Soul will come first to the Intellectual-Principle and survey all the beautiful Ideas in the Supreme and will avow that this is Beauty, that the Ideas are Beauty. For by their efficacy comes all Beauty else, but the offspring and essence of the Intellectual-Being. What is beyond the Intellectual-Principle we affirm to be the nature of Good radiating Beauty before it. So that, treating the Intellectual-Kosmos as one, the first is the Beautiful: if we make distinction there, the Realm of Ideas constitutes the Beauty of the Intellectual Sphere; and The Good, which lies beyond, is the Fountain at once and Principle of Beauty: the Primal Good and the Primal Beauty have the one dwelling-place and, thus, always, Beauty's seat is There. (1.6.9)

The Conversion of St. Paul
Acts of the Apostles

The ideas of St. Paul were totally assimilated by Augustine not long before he began writing the Confessions *in 397, and in particular Paul's understanding of grace and the bondage of the will. The conversion account of St. Paul in the "Acts of the Apostles" was also clearly in his mind when he wrote the account of his own conversion in the* Confessions.

Now Saul, still breathing threats and murder against the disciples of the Lord, went to the high priest, and asked for letters from him to the synagogues at Damascus, so that if he found any belonging to the Way, both men and women, he might bring them bound to Jerusalem. As he was traveling, it happened that he was approaching Damascus, and suddenly a light from heaven flashed around him; and he fell to the ground and heard a voice saying to him, "Saul, Saul, why are you persecuting Me?" And he said, "Who are You, Lord?" And He said, "I am Jesus whom you are persecuting, but get up and enter the city, and it will be told you what you must do." The men who traveled with him stood speechless, hearing the voice but seeing no one. Saul got up from the ground, and though his eyes were open, he could see nothing; and leading him by the hand, they brought him into Damascus. And he was three days without sight, and neither ate nor drank.

Now there was a disciple at Damascus named Ananias; and the Lord said to him in a vision, "Ananias." And he said, "Here I am, Lord." And the Lord said to him, "Get up and go to the street called Straight, and inquire at the house of Judas for a man from Tarsus named Saul, for he is praying, and he has seen in a vision a man named Ananias come in and lay his hands on him, so that he might regain his sight." But Ananias answered, "Lord, I have heard from many about this man, how much harm he did to Your saints at Jerusalem; and here he has authority from the

Scripture taken from the NEW AMERICAN STANDARD BIBLE © 1960, 1962, 1963, 1968, 1971, 1972, 1973, 1975, 1977, 1995 by The Lockman Foundation. Used with permission.

chief priests to bind all who call on Your name." But the Lord said to him, "Go, for he is a chosen instrument of Mine, to bear My name before the Gentiles and kings and the sons of Israel; for I will show him how much he must suffer for My name's sake." So Ananias departed and entered the house, and after laying his hands on him said, "Brother Saul, the Lord Jesus, who appeared to you on the road by which you were coming, has sent me so that you may regain your sight and be filled with the Holy Spirit." And immediately there fell from his eyes something like scales, and he regained his sight, and he got up and was baptized; and he took food and was strengthened.

The Grace of God
Augustine

We have seen that for Augustine, the fall of Adam and Eve resulted in the just punishment of their descendants. As such, we cannot help but sin, and our personal sins merit further punishment both in this life and in the next. Fortunately, God offers us a way out of this dilemma—the gift of his grace, which enables us to live in righteousness.

In the heavy burden that is laid upon the sons of Adam, from the day that they go out of their mothers' wombs to the day that they [die], there is found an admirable though painful monitor teaching us to be sober-minded, and convincing us that this life has become a life of punishment because of that outrageous wickedness which was perpetrated in Paradise, and that all to which the new covenant refers belongs to that future inheritance which awaits us in the world to come . . .

Now, therefore, let us walk in hope, and let us by the spirit mortify the deeds of the flesh, and so make progress from day to day. For the Lord knows those who are his; and as many as are led by the Spirit of God, they are sons of God, but by grace, not by nature. For there is but one Son of God by nature, who in His compassion became Son of Man for our sakes, so that we, by nature sons of men, might by grace become through him sons of God . . .

For as by the sin of one man we have fallen into a misery so deplorable, so by the righteousness of one man, who also is God, shall we come to a blessedness inconceivably exalted. But no one should trust that he has passed from the one man to the other until he has reached that place where there is no temptation, and has entered into the peace which he seeks in the many and various conflicts of this war, in which the flesh lusts against the spirit, and the spirit against the flesh.

Augustine. "City of God." Book 21.15-16. *Nicene and Post Nicene Father.* Vol. 2. Ed. Philip Schaff. Buffalo, NY: Christian Literature Publishing Co., 1887. Translation updated.

Now, this war would not have existed if human nature had, in the exercise of free will, continued steadfast in the uprightness in which it was created. But now in its misery it makes war upon itself, because in its blessedness it would not continue at peace with God. Though this state might be a terrible calamity, it is better than the earlier stages of this life, which do not recognize that a war is to be maintained. For it is better to struggle against vices than without struggle to be conquered by them. It is better, I say, to wage war with the hope of peace everlasting than live in captivity without any thought of deliverance. Truly, we long for the end of this war, and, kindled by the flame of divine love, we burn for entrance into that well-ordered peace in which whatever is inferior is forever subordinated to what is above it. But if (which God forbid) there had been no hope of so blessed a consummation, we should still have preferred to endure the hardness of this conflict, rather than, by our non-resistance, to yield ourselves to the dominion of vice.

Such is God's mercy towards the vessels of mercy that he has prepared for their glory. In the first age of man—that is, infancy—one submits without any resistance to the flesh. In the second age—which is called boyhood, and which has not yet understanding enough to undertake this warfare—one yields to almost every vicious pleasure . . . Yet if either of these ages has received the sacraments of the Mediator, then, even if the present life is brought to an immediate end, the child, having been translated from the power of darkness to the kingdom of Christ, shall not only be saved from eternal punishments, but shall not even suffer purgatorial torments after death. For spiritual regeneration of itself suffices to prevent any evil consequences resulting after death from the connection with death which carnal generation forms.

But when we reach that age which can now comprehend the commandment, and submit to the dominion of law, we must declare war upon vices, and wage this war keenly, lest we be led into sins meriting damnation. And if vices have not gathered strength, by habitual victory they are more easily overcome and subdued. But if they have been used to conquer and rule, it is only with difficulty and labor they are mastered. And indeed this victory cannot be sincerely and truly gained but by delighting in true righteousness, and it is faith in Christ that gives this. For if the law is present with its command, but the Sprit with its help is absent, the presence of the prohibition serves only to increase the desire to sin, and adds the guilt of transgression . . .

Vices, then, are only to be considered overcome when they are conquered by the love of God, which God himself alone gives, and which he gives only through the Mediator between God and men, the man Christ Jesus . . . But there are few indeed who are so happy as to have passed their youth without committing any damnable sins, either by dissolute or violent conduct, or by following some godless and unlawful opinions, but have subdued by their greatness of soul everything in them which could make them the slaves of carnal pleasures . . .

Whoever, therefore, desires to escape eternal punishment, let him not only be baptized, but also justified in Christ, and so let him in truth pass from the devil to Christ. And let him not fancy that there are any purgatorial pains except before that final and dreadful judgment. We must not, however, deny that even the eternal fire will be proportioned to the deserts of the wicked, so that to some it will be more, and to others less painful, whether this result is accomplished by a variation in the temperature of the fire itself, graduated according to every one's merit, or whether it is that the heat remains the same, but that all do not feel it with equal intensity of torment.

The Effects of Grace
Augustine

As Bishop of Hippo, Augustine had come to believe that the only thing human beings were capable of on their own was sin meriting eternal damnation. God's grace, however, enables human beings to avoid committing acts of personal sin, to do good works, and to have the faith necessary for salvation.

Good Works as a Gift of God's Grace

Can those who have been promised pardon and a share in the eternal kingdom . . . be restored through the merit of their own works? God forbid! For what good work can a lost man perform, except so far as he has been delivered from eternal damnation? Can he do anything by the free exercise of his own will? Again I say, God forbid. For it was by the evil use of his free-will that man destroyed both it and himself. For, as a man who kills himself must, of course, be alive when he kills himself, but after he has killed himself ceases to live, and cannot restore himself to life; so, when man by his own free-will sinned, then sin being victorious over him, the freedom of his will was lost. For of whom a man is overcome, of the same is he brought in bondage.

This is the judgment of the Apostle Peter. And as it is certainly true, what kind of liberty, I ask, can the slave possess, except when it pleases him to sin? For he is freely in bondage who does with pleasure the will of his master. Accordingly, he who is the servant of sin is free to sin. And so he will not be free to do right, until, being freed from sin, he shall begin to be the servant of righteousness. And this is true liberty, for he has pleasure in the righteous deed; and it is at the same time a holy bondage, for he is obedient to the will of God.

But from where comes this liberty to do right to the man who is in bondage and sold under sin, except insofar as he has been redeemed by Him who has said, "If the Son shall make you free,

---

Augustine. "Enchiridion." 30-32. Trans. J.F Shaw. *Nicene and Post-Nicene Fathers.* Vol. 3. Edited by Philip Schaff. Buffalo, NY: Christian Literature Publishing Co., 1887. Translation updated.

you shall be free indeed?" And before this redemption is wrought in a man, when he is not yet free to do what is right, how can he talk of the freedom of his will and his good works, except he be inflated by that foolish pride of boasting which the apostle restrains when he says, "By grace are you saved, through faith."

Faith as a Gift of God's Grace

And lest men should claim at least that faith is their own achievement, not understanding that this too is the gift of God, this same apostle, who says in another place that he had obtained mercy of the Lord to be faithful, here also adds: "And that not of yourselves; it is the gift of God: not of works, lest any man should boast." And lest it should be thought that good works will be wanting in those who believe, he adds further: "For we are his workmanship, created in Christ Jesus into good works, which God has before ordained that we should walk in them."

We shall be made truly free, then, when God fashions us, that is, forms and creates us anew, not as men—for He has done that already—but as good men, which his grace is now doing, that we may be a new creation in Christ Jesus, as it is said accordingly: "Create in me a clean heart, O God." For God had already created his heart, so far as the physical structure of the human heart is concerned; but the psalmist prays for the renewal of the life which was still lingering in his heart.

Free Will as a Gift of God's Grace

Also, should any one be inclined to boast, not indeed of his works, but of the freedom of his will, as if the first merit belonged to him, this very liberty of good action being given to him as a reward he had earned, let him listen to this same preacher of grace, when he says: "For it is God which works in you, both to will and to do of His own good pleasure; and in another place: So, then, it is not of him that wills, nor of him that runs, but of God that shows mercy."

Now as, undoubtedly, if a man is of the age to use his reason, he cannot believe, hope, love, unless he will to do so, nor obtain the prize of the high calling of God unless he voluntarily run for it. In what sense is it not of him that wills, nor of him that runs, but of God that shows mercy, except that, as it is written, the preparation of the heart is from the Lord? Otherwise, if it is said, "It is not of him that wills, nor of him that runs, but of God that shows mercy," because it is of both, that is, both of the will of man and of the mercy of God, so that we are to understand the saying, "It is not of him that wills, nor of him that runs, but of God that shows mercy," as if it meant the will of man alone is not sufficient, if the mercy of God go not with it—then it will follow that the mercy of God alone is not sufficient, if the will of man goes not with it. And therefore, if we may rightly say, it is not of man that wills, but of God that shows mercy, because the will of man by itself is not enough, why may we not also rightly put it in the converse way: It is not of God that shows mercy, but of man that wills, because the mercy of God by itself does not suffice? Surely, if no Christian will dare to say this,

It is not of God that shows mercy, but of man that wills, lest he should openly contradict the apostle, it follows that the true interpretation of the saying, "It is not of him that wills, nor of him that runs, but of God that shows mercy," is that the whole work belongs to God, who both makes the will of man righteous, and thus prepares it for assistance, and assists it when it is prepared. For the man's righteousness of will precedes many of God's gifts, but not all; and it must itself be included among those which it does not precede.

We read in Holy Scripture, both that "God's mercy shall meet me," and that "His mercy shall follow me." It goes before the unwilling to make him willing; it follows the willing to make his will effectual. Why are we taught to pray for our enemies, who are plainly unwilling to lead a holy life, unless that God may work willingness in them? And why are we ourselves taught to ask that we may receive, unless that He who has created in us the wish, may Himself satisfy the wish? We pray, then, for our enemies, that the mercy of God may prevent them, as it has prevented us: we pray for ourselves that His mercy may follow us.

Seeing God
Augustine

This brief but evocative passage from De Ordine (On Order) was written in 386, not long after Augustine's conversion. In it, Augustine attempts to describe the beatific vision, but does so in a way that seems to owe as much to Neo-Platonism as to Christian thought.

When the soul has properly adjusted and ordered itself and has transformed itself into something harmonious and beautiful, then it will be ready to see God, the source and father of all truth. O great God, what kind of eyes will those be? How pure, beautiful, powerful, constant, serene, happy! And what is it that they will see? What? I ask. What could we possibly think, believe, or say about this? Everyday words spring to mind, but they have been made trivial by being used for things of such little worth. I'll say nothing more about this except to say that what has been promised is a vision of beauty—the kind of beauty that all beautiful things imitate and, compared to which, all other things are ugly.

One who catches a glimpse of this beauty—by living, praying, and studying well—will . . . [recognize the truth] that nothing happens outside of God's plan, that all things come to pass according to that plan, and that his prayers are never in vain. And so, how could any toils, dangers, adversities, or changes of fortune ever rattle such a righteous person?

Augustine. "On Order" 2.18.51. Trans. Michael S. Russo (2019).

Eternal Happiness with God
Augustine

In the last section of his monumental work, the City of God, *Augustine describes that "eternal sabbath," in which the soul will rest forever with God. Although this passage reflects the orthodox Christian view of the afterlife, it is worth considering whether Augustine's view of the heavenly reward of the elect corresponds with what most of us believe when we think of heaven.*

How great shall that happiness be, where there will be no evil, where no good will be lacking, and where there will be leisure for praising God, who shall be all in all! For what other state can be conceived in which idleness will not sap activity nor any activity be forced by want. And yet this is precisely the state suggested by the sacred song, in which I read or hear the words, "Blessed are they that dwell in Your house, O Lord. They will praise you for ever and ever."

All the limbs and organs of the incorruptible body, which now we see to be suited to various necessary uses, shall contribute to the praises of God. For in that life necessity shall have no place, since full, certain, secure, everlasting joy will replace necessity. Further, all those parts of the bodily harmony, which are distributed through the whole body, within and without, . . . and which are hidden from our understanding, will be hidden no longer; and, along with the other great and marvelous discoveries which will then kindle rational minds in praise of the great Artist, there shall be the enjoyment of a beauty which appeals to the reason.

What sort of power of movement such bodies will possess, I'm not bold enough to attempt to define and lack the ability to even conceive. Nevertheless, I will say that in both in motion and at rest they shall be beautiful in appearance, for nothing will exist in that state which is not beautiful. One thing is certain, the body shall immediately be wherever the spirit wills, and the spirit shall will nothing which will diminish either the spirit or the body.

Augustine. "City of God." 22.30. *Nicene and Post Nicene Father.* Vol. 2. Ed. Philip Schaff. Buffalo, NY: Christian Literature Publishing Co., 1887. Translation updated.

True honor will be there, for it will be denied to no one who is worthy, nor given to anyone unworthy . . . True peace shall be there, where no one will suffer harm either from himself or any other. The reward for virtue will be God Himself, who is the author of virtue and the greatest and best of all promises . . . He will be the goal of our desires—he who we will see forever, love without cessation, praise without weariness. This state of love and action will be shared by all who participate in eternal life.

But who can imagine, let alone describe, the degrees of honor and glory that be appropriate for the various degrees of merit? Yet it cannot be doubted that there shall be degrees. Nonetheless, in that blessed city there shall be this great blessing: that no inferior shall envy any superior, just as the archangels are not envied by the angels. For no one there will wish to be what he has not been granted to be, though he will be bound in total harmony with the one to whom it has been granted . . .

The fact that they are no longer able to delight in sin, does not mean that they will have no freedom. On the contrary, the will shall be all the more truly free, because it will be set free from delight in sinning and become unfailingly fixed on delight in not sinning. The first freedom of will which man received when he was created upright consisted in an ability not to sin, but also in an ability to sin. But this last freedom will be superior, since it will bring the impossibility of sinning. This, indeed, will not be a natural ability, but the gift of God. For it is one thing to be God, another thing to be a partaker of God. God by nature cannot sin, but the partaker of God receives this inability from God.

And in this divine gift stages were to be observed. Man was first given a free will by which he was able not to sin, and at last a free will by which he was not able to sin. The first freedom was designed for the acquiring of merit, the latter to the enjoying of the reward. But, because human nature as it was first conceived sinned when it had the ability to do so, it is delivered by a more abundant grace, so as to reach that freedom in which it cannot sin.

For the first immortality which Adam lost by sinning consisted in his being able not to die; the last will consist in his not being able to die; Likewise, the first free will consisted in his being able not to sin; the last in his not being able to sin. And thus, piety and justice will be just as secure there as happiness . .

. In that heavenly city, then, there shall be free will. It will be one and the same in all and indivisible in each individual. They will be delivered from all evil, filled with all good, enjoying indefeasibly the delights of eternal joys, oblivious of sins, oblivious of sufferings, and yet not so oblivious of its deliverance as to be ungrateful to its deliverer.

The soul, then, shall have an intellectual remembrance of its past sins, but they shall be quite forgotten as far as sense experience is concerned. It will be like the skillful physician, who knows all diseases in theory, but who is ignorant of them in his personal experience, never having suffered from them . . .

Nothing will bring greater joy in that city than the celebration of the grace of Christ, who redeemed us by his blood. There the words of the psalm will be completely fulfilled: "Be still and know that I am God." There will truly be the greatest of sabbaths—the sabbath that has no evening, the sabbath that the Lord approved at the beginning of creation . . . There we will have the ability to be still, and know that He is God, whereas formerly we wished to be that ourselves, when we fell away from Him, and listened to the voice of the seducer . . . But when we are restored by him and perfected with greater grace, we will have eternal leisure to see that He is God, for we shall be full of him when he shall be all in all . . .

There we will rest and see, see and love, love and praise. This is what will be in the end without end. For what else is our purpose other than to attain to the kingdom of which there is no end?

I think I have now, by God's help, discharged my obligation in writing this large work. Let those who think I have said too little, or those who think I have said too much, forgive me; and let those who think I have said just enough join me in giving thanks to God. Amen.

For Further Reading

The Life of St. Augustine

Bonner, Gerald. *St. Augustine of Hippo: Life and Controversies.* Philadelphia: The Westminster Press, 1963.

Brown, Peter. *Augustine of Hippo.* Berkeley: Univ. of California Press, 1967.

Chadwick, Henry. *Augustine Of Hippo: A Life.* Oxford: Oxford University Press, 2009.

McCabe, Joseph. *St. Augustine and His Age.* New York: SophiaOmni, 2015.

O'Donnell, James J. *Augustine: A New Biography.* New York: Ecco, 2005.

O'Meara, John J. *The Young Augustine.* London: Longmans, Green and Co, 1954.

Wills, Gary. *St. Augustine: A Life.* New York: Penguin Books, 2005.

The Thought of Augustine

The following works are well-regarded overviews of the thought of St. Augustine that include, but are not limited to, the ideas contained in the Confessions. These works vary greatly in breadth and complexity:

Battenhouse, Roy W. *A Companion to the Study of St. Augustine.* New York: Oxford University Press, 1955.

Bourke, Vernon J. *Augustine's Quest of Wisdom.* Milwaukee, WI: Bruce Publishing Company, 1945.

—. *Augustine's View of Reality*. Villanova, PA: Villanova University Press, 1964

Clark, Mary T. *Augustine: Philosopher of Freedom*. Tournai: Desclee, 1958

Evans, G.R. *Augustine on Evil*. Cambridge: Cambridge University Press, 1982.

Gilson. Etienne. *The Christian Philosophy of St. Augustine*. Trans. L. Lynch. New York: Random House, 1960.

Harrison, Carol. *Augustine: Christian Truth and Fractured Humanity. Christian Theology in Context*. Oxford: Oxford Univ. Press, 2000.

Kirwan, Christopher. *Augustine*. London: Routledge, 1989.

Levering, Matthew. *The Theology of Augustine*. Grand Rapids. MI: Baker Publishing, 2013.

Matthews, Gareth. *Augustine*. Oxford: Blackwell, 2005.

Meconi, David and Stump, Eleonore, eds. *The Cambridge Companion to Augustine*. Cambridge: Cambridge University Press, 2014.

O'Connell, Robert J. *St. Augustine's Early Theory of Man*. Cambridge, MA: Harvard University Press, 1968.

O'Donovan, Oliver. *The Problem of Self-Love in St. Augustine*. New Haven: Yale University Press, 1980.

O'Meara, John J. *The Young Augustine*. New York: Longman's Green, 1954.

Portalié, Eugène. *A Guide to the Thought of St. Augustine*. Trans. R.J. Bastian. Chicago: Regnery, 1960.

Rist, John. *Augustine: Ancient Thought Baptized*. Cambridge: Cambridge University Press, 1994.

TeSelle, Eugene. *Augustine the Theologian. New York*: Herder and Herder, 1970.

Vessey, Mark, ed. *A Companion to the Thought of St. Augustine*. Malden, MA: John Wiley and Sons, 2012.

Confessions: Recommended Translations

The version of the Confessions *that you'll find in this study guide has been heavily edited to make it easier to read. There's no substitute, however, for reading the text in its entirety. The following translation are highly recommended both for their readability and their fidelity to the original text:*

Confessions. Trans. Maria Boulding. Hyde Park, NY: New City Press, 1997.

Confessions. Trans. Rex Warner. New York: Penguin Books, 1963.

Confessions: Commentaries

Those seeking to delve further in their study of the Confessions *are encouraged to consult the following secondary sources:*

Conybeare, Catherine. *The Routledge Guidebook to Augustine's Confessions.* New York: Routledge, 2016.

Ferrari. *The Conversion of St. Augustine.* Villanova, PA: Villanova, 1984.

Fox, Robert Lane. *Augustine: Conversions to Confessions.* New York: Perseus Books, 2015.

McMahon, Robert. *Augustine's Prayerful Ascent: An Essay on the Literary Form of the Confession.* Athens, Georgia. University of Georgia Press, 1989.

O'Connell, Robert J. *Images of Conversion in St. Augustine's Confessions.* New York: Fordham University Press, 1996.

O'Donnell, James J. *Augustine's Confessions.* 3 Vols. Oxford: Oxford University Press, 2012.

O'Meara, John J. *The Young Augustine: An Introduction to the Confessions of St. Augustine.* London: Longmans, Green, 1980.

Paffenroth, Kim and Kennedy, Robert Peter, eds. *A Reader's Companion to Augustine's Confessions*. Louisville, KY: Westminster John Knox Press, 2003.

Quinn, John M. *A Companion to the Confessions of St. Augustine*. New York: Peter Lang, 2002.

Rigby, Paul. *The Theology of Augustine's Confessions*. Cambridge: Cambridge University Press, 2015.

Starnes, Colin. *Augustine's Conversion*. Waterloo, Ontario: Wilfred Laurier University Press.1990.

Vaught, Carl G. *The Journey Towards God in Augustine's Confessions: Books I-IV*. Albany, NY: State University of New York Press, 2003.

—. *Encounters with God in Augustine's Confessions: Books VII-IX*. Albany, NY: State University of New York Press, 2004.

—. *Access to God in Augustine's Confessions: Books X-XIII*. Albany, NY: State University of New York Press, 2004.

Wills, Gary. *Augustine's Confessions*. Princeton, NJ: Princeton University Press, 2011.

Other Essential Works of St. Augustine

The following are excellent translations of some of Augustine's most notable works apart from the Confessions. *The complete Augustinian canon is massive, but any of these works would be a good starting point for those seeking to continue their exploration of Augustine's writings:*

The Augustine Catechism: The Enchiridion on Faith, Hope, and Charity (Enchiridion ad Laurentium). Hyde Park, NY: New City Press, 1999.

The City of God Against the Pagans (De Civitate Dei). Trans. R.W. Dyson. Cambridge: Cambridge University Press, 1998.

On Christian Teaching (De Doctrina Christiana). Oxford: Oxford University Press, 1997.

Divine Providence and the Problem of Evil (De Ordine). Fathers *of the Church Series.* Trans. Ludwig Schopp. Washington, D.C., Catholic University of America Press, 1948.

Grace and Free Will (De Gratia et Libero Arbitrio). Fathers of the Church Series. Trans. Robert P. Russell. Washington, D.C., Catholic University of America Press, 1968.

On Free Choice of the Will (De Libero Arbitrio). Trans. Thomas Williams. Indianapolis, IN: Hackett Publishing, 1993.

The Happy Life (De Beata Vita). Fathers of the Church Series. Trans. Ludwig Schopp. Washington, D.C., Catholic University of America Press, 1948.

The Trinity (De Trinitate). Trans. Edmund Hill. Hyde Park, NY: New City Press, 1991.